PERspective

PROS AND CONS OF EXPAT LIFE – EXPERIENCES FROM 25 YEARS AND 84 COUNTRIES

By Per Ostberg

FIRST EDITION PUBLISHED BY PER OSTBERG, MARCH 2014

Printed by CreateSpace, an Amazon.com Company and available from Amazon.com, CreateSpace.com, and other retail outlets

Catalogue records for this book are available from the National Library, Stockholm, Sweden, and via the Swedish ISBN agency on: www.kb.se/isbn-centralen/sok-forlagsregistret/

ISBN: 978-91-981685-0-1 (pbk.)

ISBN: 978-91-981686-0-0 (ebook)

Cover photograph © Tul Sing Gurung

Author photograph © Richard Humphries

Cover design and illustration © Greg Cameron & Zahné Briel

www.PerOstberg.com

To Cherry: for being such a princess and showing such patience with all my wild ideas. Life wouldn't be the same without you!

ACKNOWLEDGEMENTS

My grateful thanks to Lars-Åke Ohlén for the use of his sofa, Herrn Dr Urs Ammann for letting me work at Oerlikon-Contraves, Per Englund for taking Mike Danilovic's call, Monica Jansson, Magnus Holmgren and Mats Hultman at Ericsson for all their support, TY Hsii for his fantastic leadership, George Aylmer for persuading me to come to Egypt, Thomas Jonell for sending me to Sierra Leone during a civil war, David van Staden, Chris Kruger, and their families for their warm hospitality, Moez Day, Franco Ricotta, Gretchen Helmer, Kamiel Koot, Nick Kamperdijk, and Alan Gray for their buoyancy and enthusiasm.

Thanks to Marjo Baayen, Philippe Ambonguilat, Tim Furness, Praveena Raman, Dirk Lourens, Stepahno Furahino and the Celtel Tanzania Project crew for being the best team ever. You guys rock!

My thanks also go to Wayne Nelson-Esch for his crazy idea, Nix Nolledo, Raymond Racaza and Andy Garcia from Xurpas for taking a chance on Wayne and me, Dominic Leong for being such a cool dude, Michelle Leal, Jonathan Hoehler and the Starfish Mobile staff, Nigel Jacobs for his gift of the gab, my mother, Birgitta Svanholm, and sister, Karin Ostberg for their encouragement, Tul Sing Gurung for his amazing photo on Ama Dablam, Caroline Hurry for casting a critical eye over my manuscript. PERspective could not have happened without you all.

TABLE OF CONTENTS

INTRODUCTION

The travel bug bit me early. Burying myself in the pages of Jules Verne, Ernest Hemingway, or James Michener marked my adolescence. From *Biggles* to *Seven Years in Tibet*, any book set in an exotic place inspired my desire to see the world. And I have. My 25-year journey has taken me to more than 80 countries, via winding roads and back alleys with cul-de-sacs. And I haven't hung up my rucksack yet.

As a Swedish expat first starting out, I had nothing to prepare me for some of the culture shocks that lay in store. Nobody handed me a no-holds-barred overview of working for a multinational in a foreign country, I had to figure out my own footpath and stumble along. Ups and downs combined with meeting amazing people, learning a ton and having loads of fun.

The experiences I describe in this book are my own. The idea to write it all down came to me while I was in Taipei in the late 90s comforting a colleague from our Swedish head office. I handed her a tissue as she sobbed and spluttered.

"Sorry, I needed to let that out," she sniffed, looking embarrassed.

"What's up?" I asked. I could see the staff outside my miniscule office giving us odd looks.

"Nothing … everything," she said. "I don't know what I'm doing here."

She had been in Taiwan for about a fortnight and had about three months to go before she was due back in Sweden.

"I don't know what's expected of me," she added. "Everyone looks to me for direction but I'm not here to train or manage people. I don't know this place. I'm not a manager but even the real manager just looks to me for advice."

I handed her a cup of coffee.

"There is nothing wrong with you," I said. "It's a classic case of culture crash."

Expats abroad go through phases. At first, you do not understand the country. It is all new and exciting and you are coping well. Then you start to learn how the country works. You pick up on how the locals think. You start to appreciate the nuances. You think you've figured it out. Then one day, after around three months in the country – WHAM! Nothing you thought you understood makes any sense. It's the culture crash. Do not fool yourself; it hits everyone! The more aware you are, the less it will hurt.

I told her about my own culture crash, sitting on St Kilda's beach outside Melbourne that saw me drizzling drunkenly over the phone to a friend in Sweden. I had no one to talk to in Melbourne. She said her rainy Taipei trauma beat my Melbourne misery hands down. I could have raised her an emergency Sierra Leone evacuation but I was not trying to score points.

Later that night over beers with friends we discussed the expatriate lifestyle, the vast differences in values between national and organisational cultures and how work expectations from local management differed from the home organisations. We all felt our respective companies could have done more to train and prepare us.

In PERspective, I show the flip side of expatriate lifestyle and give an honest description of how life could look. As examples and illustrations, I use my own mistakes, victories and experiences. There's a Swedish slant to how I interpret various situations and the backdrop is the telecom industry, but the issues and reflections are universal.

The expatriate situations I cover include the business trip, short-term overseas assignment, long-term contract and progression from working for a foreign multi-national to starting your own company overseas.

Professor Geert Hofstede's and Fons Trompenaars' intercultural management theories are discussed briefly as a framework. Then there is all the messy human stuff – relationships, sex, drugs, rock 'n' roll, possible pitfalls, roads to hell paved with good intentions. I have tried to be realistic without taking refuge in political correctness.

I worked five years for Ericsson in the late 90s, fine-tuning the logistic flow between Sweden and its subsidiaries in Asia for mobile network rollout projects. It was an amazing experience, providing unprecedented opportunities, freedom, and authority to break new ground. As my experience evolved, I built mobile networks in six African countries for Celtel International, a Dutch holding company, over three years and built up Starfish Mobile, a pan-African mobile valued-added services company with operations in 21 countries, for 11 years.

I've walked with giraffes on the Niger savannah, played golf during sandstorms in Chad, lived through a civil war in Sierra Leone and got drunk with ex SAS soldiers at Paddy's bar in Freetown. I've climbed Kilimanjaro, swam with dolphins outside Pemba, deep-sea fished outside Zanzibar and been locked up for hours at immigration in the Ivory Coast. I've woken up naked on a beach in Koh Phangan after a four-day full moon party and driven a dugout canoe up and down the Kinabatangan River in Borneo.

I have taken over 650 flights and done 54 laps around the world in miles flown and spent more than six months in airports and airplanes.

If you're wondering what it's like to throw caution to the wind and embrace a new world of travel, adventure, and exploration in a foreign country, read on. Whether you dream of living your own jet set lifestyle or if your staff have to travel around the world; this book is for you!

Knowing what I do now, I would have still done the same and jumped on that first plane!

LIVING THE DREAM

"Travel is fatal to prejudice, bigotry, and narrow mindedness." – Mark Twain

Ah, the joys of travel! Don't you just love the new smells, the sights, sounds, and everything else – ok, the immigration officials, not so much – that traversing foreign countries entails? I'd wanted to explore the world for as long as I could remember. As a youngster I enjoyed nothing more than lugging a backpack around Swedish forests, mountain climbing, sailing the southern coasts, or skiing in the Alps. As soon as I was old enough I left for Asia.

Sometimes you need to let go and trust. En route to Phuket and Phi Phi Islands, my friend decided to return to Sweden for a job interview. I drifted on with vague plans of getting to Indonesia and ended up driving tourists up and down the Kinabatangan River in northeast Borneo. My partner was a 35hp outboard engine propelling the dugout through the rapids.

I wore flip-flops and surf shorts to work. T-shirt optional. The place was magical with its deep, dark, rainforest, chattering cicadas and remote villages filled with kind, respectful people, who depended on the river for their livelihoods but not long after I left, the virgin jungle was torn down in the name of progress. Today a logging trail along the Kinabatangan River has turned much of its clear, fish-filled waters into a muddy streak.

After a study trip to Hong Kong, Guangzhou, Seoul and Tokyo, I spent eight months backpacking in South East Asia – seeing as much as I could by day and partying hard at night.

Arriving at Khao San Road, Bangkok, where backpackers hung out in droves, in '92 was electrifying. Well do I recall those musky tropical smells, rattling ceiling fans, passionate all-nighters heard through cardboard-thin walls and the tasty Thai food. Each restaurant had a blaring TV with scheduled shows.

Shops selling everything from exotic spices to cheap fabrics spilled onto the pavements, rubbing shoulders with tattoo parlours, and bars offering Singha beers or Mekong and Cokes. Tuk-Tuks weaved in and out of the chaotic traffic, amid car, bike, and ganja fumes. We wore dreadlocks, baggy shorts, batik trousers, and faded T-shirts. The shabbier you looked, the cooler you were. Showing a guidebook was a no-no. Only the new arrivals clutched *Lonely Planet* guidebooks. We, the travel veterans, told each other about the good places, the untouched spots. That's how the true travellers got around.

Think bombed-out, one-dollar-a-night, reed huts on island beaches in Thailand, with a hole in the roof above a hard, damp, mattress. Bargain! A long soak in the clear blue ocean five metres away cures a hangover from the buckets of local hooch gulped down the night before. Small coral fish nibble on your toes. The whiff of grilled fish assails your nostrils as a beach vendor weaves towards you. Music blares from the hole in the wall pub. Ahhhh, it's just another day in paradise.

Such is your perspective as a callow youth starting out. Sadly, those early backpacking days are no more. No longer can you hire a motorbike in Vietnam for a few dollars without papers, and just leave it for the owner's cousin at a restaurant in Da Nang, four days riding north. Gone are the days when you rocked up at an airport in Borneo, chatted to the pilot, got a jump seat in the cockpit and saw the jungles roll by far below or when 10 dollars sorted out your visa on arrival in some unknown African airport.

HOW TO GET OVERSEAS

There are always opportunities. It is up to you to grab them. Take my friend who sells properties in a ski resort in central Sweden, for example. In January and February, after families from Stockholm have spent a fantastic Christmas and New Year there, the fathers fly in to buy apartments. In April and May, after the Easter holiday, fathers come back to sell their places. In a good year, he can sell the same unit twice. The rest of the year, he goes diving in South East Asia. The sales commissions pays for his lifestyle.

Travelling can be very expensive but if your dream is to see the world and if you're determined enough, I believe fate conspires to bring about desired events. My own journey started something like this:

"You're hired!"

I coughed into my coffee mug. "What?"

"Don't you want to work for us?" Per Englund smiled. He knew I was keen. Per worked for the department within Ericsson Radio Systems AB handling sales and implementation of GSM mobile networks for South East Asia. We had met through an Intercultural Management course, while I was an assistant teacher, just back from my year drifting in Asia.

"What do you want me to do?" I asked.

"Just logistics," he said.

Logistics? What the devil were those? I'd have to read up sharpish.

"When do you want me to start?"

"Yesterday, already. We have some big projects coming up," said Per.

"I'll call you tomorrow," I said, my mind racing.

I set off at a gallop to the Finance Institution at our local university to pick the brain of a girlfriend doing her PhD in Logistics. I held up a hand as she tried to explain the theory to me. It all sounded far too complicated.

"Stop. Make it shorter. Explain logistics in three minutes. Go!"

"Assume you have a box at point A that needs to go to point B. In between is C and D. Logistics is moving the box to B as cheaply as possible – say via customs, shipping and airlines with full control," she said.

"I can do that," I decided. So begun my first step on the first rung of my multi-national ladder. All it took was a little luck, timing and naive trust in the unknown!

THE PROS AND CONS OF BUSINESS TRIPS

"Sir?"

I stirred at the gentle tap on my shoulder and opened a bleary eye. The Thai Airways flight attendant held a food tray. The smell of coffee and airline breakfast hung in the air.

"Breakfast?" she asked.

"No, thanks, we just took off," I grumbled.

"No sir, we start our descent to Stockholm in 15 minutes."

"What?" I stretched and disentangled myself from the blanket.

"What do you do? Are you a pilot?" the guy next to me blurted out.

"No. Why?" I answered through a mouthful of scrambled eggs.

"Even when we clambered over you, you didn't stir. The flight attendants have been giggling and fussing over you all night!"

Soon after we had left Bangkok, I had fallen asleep. The flight attendants had removed my spectacles, reclined my seat, propped a pillow behind my head and tucked me in with a blanket. I had slept 14 hours straight in economy class. I was on the way back to Sweden from the third trip to South East Asia that month.

The last 25 years, I have taken over 650 flights and flown the equivalent of 54 laps around the world. I have spent more than six months in airports and airplanes and nearly eight years in hotels or guesthouses in over 80 countries.

I have flown back home to Sweden from Philippines on a Thursday for a planned weekend with friends. On arrival in the office on Friday morning, I was told to be in Taiwan for a presentation on

Saturday. Back in the plane, I went! Presentation held, bottle of wine drunk in hotel room, pass out, wake up, check out, taxi, check in, immigration and customs, Hong Kong, new flight, airplane dinner, movie, pass out, wake up, airplane breakfast, land, immigration, taxi, apartment, subway, office. Thank God, it is Monday again!

I am fortunate. I can sleep anywhere. I have flown with colleagues who cannot sleep on planes at all. Initially I felt bad but always just apologised, and fell asleep. It was how I coped with the Sweden - South East Asia commuting. Flew on weekends! Slept all the way!

TRAVEL POLICIES

Travel policies have become an important factor in an expat's life.

At Ericsson, my department's policy was that if you travelled in Europe, you travelled business class. If you did the intercontinental flights, you flew economy, unless you were an upper manager. It all came down to money. You could do four trips to South East Asia in economy instead of just one in business.

There were, of course, loopholes. Some colleagues always flew business. It depended on timing, pre-planning and pre-booking.

When building mobile networks in Africa, Celtel International's policy was to fly business. In Africa, it made sense, at least before 9/11. We carried on all our stuff – no lost luggage, hanging around at the carousel or theft from bags at airports.

Flight policies aside, you have accommodation and allowance policies to consider. The higher the job grade, the better the hotel rooms, a club floor possibly, with breakfast and free drinks in the afternoon. With a long stay, you might be able to get a clubroom. And so on.

As a working traveller, you need to understand the policies and make them work for you. Simple assumptions without ascertaining the facts can create impossible expectations. If you relocate to another country or start with a new company, the rules will likely change.

In the beginning, you'll jump at every opportunity to fly somewhere. The company's trust that you'll get the job done feels awesome. And how cool is it to see new places while you build your career? Business travel can affect all aspects of your lifestyle. Some succeed. Some get stuck. Some get out in time. Everyone experiences different challenges. Mine was finding great bed linen. You'd expect to find high thread-count Egyptian cotton sheets in Egypt, but sadly, I never did!

Another challenging aspect of business travel is countering the effect of time zones. If you fly from Stockholm to the Philippines, you arrive the afternoon of the next day. In Sweden, weekends are sacred, so we tend to start the business trip on Mondays. To be back for a weekend in Sweden from Manila you need to leave Friday morning latest. You still only get to Stockholm on Saturday morning. You will have spent the whole week traveling for two days work in Philippines. Add religious holidays in other countries and you could easily waste a week, accomplishing nothing.

Constant hurtling from one meeting to another between time zones soon takes the fun out of flying. Everything segues into a grey sameness. The office in Taipei looks the same as the office in Indonesia. All resemble the head office. One hotel blurs into another, each with a depressing sense of *déjà vu*. For some this is reassuring, but I prefer variation. I like to feel and see that I am in a different place. Sameness becomes boring for me.

Before 9/11, airports were more fun, relaxed, a place to meet people. Now all the security checks, visa requirements, long queues and endless hours waiting have taken all the fun out of flying.

As Swedes, we have always been luckier than most. Most countries open their doors to Swedes *sans* visas with minimum fuss. Not so for most other nationalities, who have to produce bank statements, confirmed hotel bookings, cash on hand, letter of invitations, reference letters from current employers for their personal interview at the embassy, just to get a two-week visa for

UK, Sweden or France. The red tape beggars belief and more often than not, they get turned down for no good reason.

Now it seems the Swedes have to swallow the same medicine. Unlike early 2000 when you could just rock up in Africa with a ticket, a passport, some cash, and a handwritten note, Europeans now need visas for Africa too. Sauce for the goose, and all that.

Oh, wait! Did I mention office envy? Ridiculous, I know, but it's more common than you might think. Some of my colleagues, who had been in the job for 20 years with more experience than me, resented my travel perks. At the same time, they did not believe local staff could do the job. If you encounter office envy, simply rise above it. It's their problem, not yours.

With all the above pitfalls, we still do it because travel offers intoxicating challenges. Trips are characterised by achievements. You solve problems. Get the job done. Sign the contract. Decide on the way forward. Sell concepts. Present a product. You can talk over the phone to your counterparts or email but nothing beats face-to-face meetings. Certain tasks are impossible to achieve remotely.

Visiting the client will build up a relationship and help solve any miscommunication problems. It is important to connect and feel that you are both part of the same team.

If you work hard, you can rise to a position where you can cherry pick your trips.

TAKE A CHANCE ON ME

About six months into the planning and preparation for the Taiwan network rollouts, I returned to our head office in Stockholm.

"You look tired," said our finance controller, Gabrielle Wessel, as we sipped coffee from the machine.

"Yeah. It's been hectic."

"Can the Taiwanese handle it?" she asked.

I shrugged. The trips were taking their toll. I felt drained and had a constant caffeine shake. "I don't know. We have to make it work somehow," I mused.

Robert Linnarsson, our department boss three levels above me, joined the discussion. "Tell me your thoughts, Per."

"When we decided to let Taiwan order equipment for themselves, we won three new contracts though we were only aiming for one," I said. "We have to roll out three parallel networks and oversee the flow of equipment all the way to the sites. We can order entire equipment kits instead of bits and pieces now, but without close co-ordination, we could be setting them up for failure. The project managers don't understand the new structure."

"Can't we do it from Stockholm?" Robert asked.

"Not with Sweden's employment cap," I said. "We can't control the warehousing and site deliveries, neither can we support the local project managers from here. And I doubt the supply division is trained enough to manage 120 tons of equipment arriving every week!"

Robert rubbed his chin. "What do we need?" he asked.

Me, I thought! I wanted a formal overseas posting with its higher salary and associated benefits. I threw it out there. "You need on the ground support for the supply division, someone who knows the systems and equipment. You need an ambitious project manager for the nationwide network roll-out. Let me help TY Hsii and his supply division start everything up. Base me there for six months." Nothing ventured, right …

"I'll think about it," said Robert.

The following week my boss called me in. I was moving to Taiwan for seven months! A coffee chat had changed my life!

PERKS OF BUSINESS TRAVEL

"A 20% increase just for moving to Taiwan?" I asked Ericsson's HR person.

"Yes, for increased living expenses. It's taxable but if you stay outside of Sweden more than six months, it should be tax free." She sounded a bit vague. "We also pay reasonable expenses – laundry, transport, and so on – according to Ericsson Taiwan's policies."

"Do you have them?"

"No, you need to get them when you arrive."

Note to self: Check on taxation and local policies.

Amazing, I thought. Ericsson is paying me extra to experience Asia, a region I love. Bar the work, it felt like paid vacation. Getting paid to travel, what a bonus!

Different companies use different structures for business trips. Some use Per Diems, others use 'all-expense paid' structures.

For short-term contracts there is usually a percentage salary increase based on the increased living expenses while being away.

The more complex long-term contracts cover various expat benefits. Structured salaries are common with a taxable local portion and a tax-free overseas portion. Salary levels vary with job grading but also with the country's hardship factor and cost of living indexes. On the plus side, housing, cars, schooling, home trips, moving costs, work permits for spouses, and similar lifestyle costs are important factors. Too many expats looked only at the "great salary" without considering all the other costs. Do not fall into that trap. It is expensive to live in another country!

SINK OR SWIM

In Taiwan, I had an office, a project team, and shared a secretary with the division manager. Compared to my open-plan desk two management levels down in Sweden, I had done pretty well. I was negotiating with the Taiwanese customs' head honchos, meeting with division and project managers, sitting in on client meetings, presenting status reports. It felt good. There was just one catch. With no formal managerial experience, I had to learn on the job.

Compensating for my lack of skills with long hours, bold decisions, and requests for help, I dived in to the deep end. Thanks to the invaluable support from my fantastic home manager, Monica Jansson, and local manager TY Hsii, things went swimmingly. I wanted to be in Taiwan. I had to succeed. I was hungry to advance my career.

Getting tossed into turbulent waters is common. Coming from the HQ, expectations on you are high. You must be both expert and problem solver, do-er and manager. The exposure to higher management is great and you can advance your career fast. Failing will lead to a desk back home. Forever!

GO FOR WHAT YOU WANT, EVEN IF IT DOESN'T WORK OUT

I spoke a lot to my manager in Sweden, Monica Jansson, about how the constant flying between Asia and Sweden took its toll on friends, family, and potential girlfriends. I had started a relationship with Ivanna, a girl I had met in Jakarta en route to Taiwan. I wanted to give the relationship a chance but the cross-continent commuting wasn't helping.

The work we had done in Taiwan was a success and my managers wanted to continue with other countries. Several big GSM contracts were coming up. I asked Monica if I could be based in Indonesia so that I could spend time with Ivanna. Naturally, I highlighted all the positives for the company – no issues with time difference, cheaper and quicker regional flights, and constant in-country support – and she agreed.

Arriving in Jakarta, mouldy tropical smells mixed with clove cigarettes hit me as we walked up the concourse to immigration. I would spend a year in this tropical paradise. A couple of big Ericsson contracts were on the way in and we wanted to finish restructuring the logistics and supply chain for Ericsson Indonesia.

I hit the ground running. I had to get a car, a driver, new laptop, cell phone, office, meet my staff, the project team, and strike alliances with new managers plus locate nightspots and restaurants. Within 30 days, I found a three-bedroomed mansion to rent. The pool was larger than my Swedish apartment. Happy days!

The first months whipped by. The excitement faded. It was just another job, albeit in paradise. Normality set in. Exploring new shops, places and restaurants lost the exotic allure and life become mundane. In the long run, the relationship with Ivanna didn't survive the lifestyle and three countries later it crashed.

While most of my friends were married with their first or second baby on the way, Ivanna and I drifted apart. When I told her I was going to Sierra Leone for six months, she told me to keep going … so I did.

IN SHORT

- Pursue your dreams. Make them happen, no matter how wild or far-flung they seem. Dreams make us human.
- Life's too short for regrets, so just do it.
- Before you set out, read up on the taxation rules as well as local policies.
- Explore! Experience! Learn! Have fun! Live!

A TYPICAL DAY - PROBLEM, SOLUTION, NEXT!

"The measure of success is not whether you have a tough problem to deal with, but whether it is the same problem you had last year." — John Foster Dulles, Former US Secretary of State

After close to 20 years of international management experience, I've humbly realised there's a lot I could have done better. I've paid my school fees and picked up some important lessons. My top four are:

- be available and accessible,
- act with integrity and honesty,
- understand everyone reacts differently to situations,
- take decisions and lead by example.

Availability

If you're the boss, there's no excuse for not being available when your staff need you. I can't stress that enough. No matter where you are or what you're doing, even if it's 3 am in your country and a chat is the last thing you feel like, if you have staff in the field somewhere, you have to be available 24/7.

I learnt this through experience. After a car crash in Jakarta, I tried to call my manager but got only his voice mail. On another occasion when we had to evacuate in a hurry from Sierra Leone, my managers in Holland did not answer their phones.

Things happen when you sleep. You just have to wake up and deal with them! You are the manager and your employees need your decisions and guidance. If you respect your staff, they will not abuse your accessibility by random calls in the middle of the night.

Honesty and Integrity

Are there any more important human qualities than integrity and honesty in business? Not in my book. Sure, acting with integrity could earn you flak and management might even sacrifice you for it, but you will walk away with your head held high.

Many managers and expats will discover that it's just a question of time until a supplier offers you a bribe. More commonly, it's an official requesting one. The financial incentive can be huge but it really isn't worth it. I never took any proffered incentives but I know of guys who did, and lived to regret it. If somebody bribes you, he owns you. Just don't go there!

Accept Differences

On the surface, we might look and act alike, but deep down we are all different. In order to succeed you have to accept this, adapt to it, and act upon it. The further you stray from your own culture, the larger the differences are. As an expat, you will be part of, or managing, a multi-cultural team. Embrace the differences and make them work for you.

Take Decisive Action

An indecisive manager is hell to work for or even just to be around. Yes, some decision makers step on toes or will sacrifice anything and anyone for progress, but I'd still rather work for one of them than someone who sits on the fence. If there's a positive result despite their inefficiency, they are always the first to claim all the glory.

If you've been posted overseas in a managerial capacity you are expected to lead by example so take sharp decisive decisions. Decisiveness is the path to success.

WHO DARES WINS

To show you how a typical day in an expat's life might look, allow me to share some of my own experiences.

Being geographically diverse, Ericsson faced some complex delivery problems – capacity constraints from airlines and time constraints for sea freight. We manufactured most electronics in Sweden and bought from suppliers all over the world. While the shipping department was in Stockholm, local organisations interfaced daily with clients and implemented the networks with the equipment we sent from head office.

We had to run the gamut of customs requirements – different from project to project and country to country. Electronic components came as a collection of separate cards. Non-electronics came in bits and pieces – screws, nuts, cables, clamps and ties. If you needed a computer cabinet, you had to specify various quantities of 16 or 18 different items. Each piece had to be individually priced otherwise it was stuck in customs.

We bought copper cables and steel ladders in Scotland, which we airfreighted via Stockholm to East Asia. We sent sensitive electronics in containers. We used all the space we could find to get the kit to its destinations. There were constant client changes or adjustments from the project team on the ground, which resulted in warehouses full of unused equipment. The clients always blamed us for being late. And Ericsson still made a hefty profit.

An ancient, inflexible mainframe ordering system – phones, faxes, binders of equipment breakdown lists and the like – all made for a highly inefficient workflow. The project teams on the ground had to rely on faxed Excel sheets for equipment arrival information. It was madness.

I was the new guy in town. I got the easiest market, or so everyone thought. Ericsson's well-run company in Australia locally sourced and assembled equipment before delivering to the client. They only bought electronics from head office. Without access to the online ordering systems, they too, were dependent on faxed Excel sheets. They bought a lot of both fixed line and the GSM units from Ericsson.

I handled the GSM side and Ericsson Australia accounted for most of our department's turnover. The Commercial Manager and I worked around the clock on a whole lot of stupid stuff such as Australians sending requests to the wrong unit in Sweden with incorrect part numbers, for example. We had to answer questions about delivery times, pricing, and technical specifications or rewrite shipping documents based on client changes. It was messy, boring, repetitive work.

Feeling frustrated over a coffee with Per Englund, my boss, I vented: "Why can't they look in the bloody systems themselves? All information they need is there."

Per mulled it over. "Yeah. Why don't they?" he agreed. As Per phoned his data systems colleagues, I walked back to my desk, wondering if I might see my friends that night or whether they had given up on me. It was a Friday, after all.

Twenty minutes later, Per popped his head around the potted palm.

"Let's go." He was hopping from foot to foot.

I indicated the pile of folders on my desk with a sigh.

"Leave it. We have work to do," he said.

That afternoon we outlined a plan to transform the way Ericsson worked with its local companies in South East Asia without all the time-consuming, non-core logistics work. While local companies had access to Ericsson's global private data network linking them to head office, they lacked three things – system access, system knowledge, and a printer that could interpret the data from the ordering system.

The latter turned out to be the hardest part to solve, silly as it sounds today. The rest was training – and lots of it. Sure, we needed some approvals and high-level strategic decisions, as well as the buy-in from the local companies and our department boss. These were minor details. We had to move the logistic knowledge base from our department to each local company's supply division or project team. This was, of course, six years before the IT boom provided a multitude of online distributed ordering systems.

Moral of the story: Speak up – you never know where an offhand comment may lead.

DELIVERING THE ELEVATOR PITCH

Most trips and meetings are like elevator pitches. You have an hour or two to sell your idea or product. You might have flown across continents for a meeting. If you cannot close the deal, you will have wasted your time. Forget about Lady Luck bailing you out, you need to be prepared and know your stuff.

As Gary Player once said, "The more I practice, the luckier I get."

In order to make changes on the fly, you need to understand your client's business, understand how your product or idea can solve his problems. The number of unprepared people flying around who cannot even answer questions about their own products is sad to see. What a missed opportunity once interest has waned.

"Erm … Per? Just a second, please." Claes Ödman, Ericsson's negotiation leader, interrupted my presentation within a couple of minutes.

I was trying to explain how Ericsson would handle the logistic processes and flow of material to the proposed network in Taiwan. Had I cocked it up? Already?

"Gentlemen," Claes continued. "I spoke to Per yesterday before he flew from Sweden. Some things have since changed since then. Let's take a short break while I fill him in."

Things had changed? This was news to me.

"How are you?" asked Claes, looking at my caffeine-shaking hands.

"Ok, I guess. On my 10th cup of coffee," I replied, gulping down another mouthful. I had left Philippines on the Thursday and arrived in Sweden on the Friday morning. Seven hours later, I was on a plane back to Asia, working on my presentation during the flight and connecting to Taiwan in Hong Kong. On landing in Taipei, I gave the secretary a disk with the presentation, checked in, had a shower, and took out a clean shirt.

Now we were in the 28th floor boardroom with a great view of Taipei on a wet Saturday afternoon. The rain coming down from the mountains reflected a myriad of glittering Chinese ads and billboards on the wet roads traversed by thousands of scooters, bikes, and cars. I wanted an office like this!

"Sorry, everything changed while you were flying – payment terms, responsibility splits, timelines, even scope," said Claes and dove into the details. "Can you adjust the presentation?" he concluded.

"Yeah," I sighed. I gulped down an 11th cup of coffee, found some paper, and walked back into the meeting.

I looked at our potential clients – average age 55 – sitting around the table. They had been in the shipping business for decades. I was 30 with two years of logistics experience with Ericsson. I had to tell these experts how we were going to do it better than they could. We wanted control of the equipment from origin to its destination on the various sites all over Taiwan. We wanted to manage the variations and the 40 or so different suppliers with different lead-times. Our potential clients wanted to handle it themselves to save costs using their established shipping channels.

Showtime, folks! I took a deep breath.

"Gentlemen. May I have the presentations back, please?" Demonstratively I threw them into the bin and attacked the whiteboard as I explained about the ordering set-up at Ericsson Taiwan, local purchasing, the handling of equipment, customs, warehousing, site deliveries, warranty swaps, shipping co-ordination, payment, and insurance terms. I was on fire!

On Monday morning – 48 hours later – I walked into the offices in Stockholm. I looked like shit, my manager told me, but we got the contract. With gritty eyes, I went home and slept for two days.

Treat every meeting as an elevator pitch and you'll find you can handle anything!

WHEN MISUNDERSTANDINGS ARISE

"It's not about the people. It's about the game," as Gordon Gekko said in *Wall Street* (1987)

There may be times when the game rules suddenly change. Nobody bothers to tell you, and you'll cast covetous eyes at the reserve bench. Times when you'll find yourself dodging verbal bullets and wonder how this happened.

"Are you serious?"

Looking across the vast desk at Birger Flygare, a Swede and vice president of Ericsson Taiwan in charge of GSM network contracts, and George Aylmer, an American and Ericsson's project director for our largest client, FarEastone, I couldn't believe my ears.

"If we don't think you've done a good job, we cannot recommend you for the next posting," Birger answered. I had heard them right.

"Have I done a bad job?" I asked in bewilderment.

"You are not managing the equipment deliveries properly. There are delays. Our client is not happy," said Birger.

"But there are no sites to put the equipment on yet," I protested. "The client knows that. They are responsible for giving us sites. And they have seen the delivery schedule."

"Yes, but they want to see equipment here," George said. "They want more detailed reports."

Added Birger: "We don't think you understand how important this is. We don't think you are focused on this project."

This was going from bad to worse. Birger had been part of the discussion around the logistic process changes. He had also approved the project. Now he was back-pedalling.

Fuming, I later sat down with TY Hsii, the supply division boss, and discussed Birger and George's criticisms. Then I called my boss in Sweden to ask her advice. The cause of the misunderstanding was the various opinions on what my job entailed.

Home management explained my roles in Taiwan to George and Birger and eventually, the issue was resolved. The changes in the supply chain worked, the local team did a sterling job servicing the network rollout projects, I got a new posting, and everyone was happy. But for a while it was touch and go. One misunderstanding can slam your career to a grinding halt!

TAKING THE RAP!

Change is the only constant. However, for many people change can upset routines, shift corporate power structures, and threaten the status quo. Sometimes you will have to play the role of the scapegoat. Sometimes you will be hung out to dry.

Your performance is based on how well your subordinates, peers, and superiors across the organisation deal with the changes you try to implement. My work, changing the supply chain for Ericsson's GSM projects, affected our internal GSM equipment-manufacturing units, suppliers in Sweden, our shipping department, local business units and the scope of local project organisations.

Changes in the supply chain were initiated from Ericsson's head office to cut staff costs, simplify processes, minimize the warehouse surpluses, and cut lead-times. In my mind, my role was clear: Take control, change the procedures, buy local materials where applicable, train the local staff, hand over, and then leave.

Simple? You'd think, but it wasn't. Firstly, the local company and home office passed the bill back and forth until a shared cost model between head office, local company and the project was eventually agreed on.

Secondly, issues were raised about the roles of supply division managers. The project team wanted to know how they would get service and priority. Again, nobody wanted to pick up the bill.

Thirdly, as I took control of the material flow, transport arrangement, customs and project managerial tasks, I had to get involved in client meetings, something I had not done before and something I had no experience of. Boy - did I have to learn fast!

Being the junior guy in charge of equipment supply, I had to take the blame for why Ericsson could not deliver in time. When management then also forbid you to tell the truth, it can be a very uncomfortable position indeed.

"Why has the material been delayed?" the client asked.

That was the very question our managing director had forbidden me to answer but instead of stepping in and taking over the discussion, he just looked at me expectantly. You could have cut the silence with a knife. I was damned either way. I decided to tell the truth. Bad move. Back in the office, I got a good dressing down.

What can I say? Life is not always fair.

A week after I arrived in Cairo to service our new client, Glick GSM, the same question arose.

"When is the material coming?"

"I have no idea," I replied.

"What? You have no idea?" I could hear how unimpressed our client, Neil, was. The material situation was catastrophic. The few things ordered had lead times six months out. No one in the Ericsson team knew what was needed and we were supposed to launch in a couple of months.

Once again, there was no help forthcoming from my managers sitting around the table.

"Give me two weeks. Then I'll know," I answered. Later I got another lecture on what not to say to clients but they held their tongues when I showed them the magnum of Moët that Neil gave me later to say "Thank-you for the accurate and timely deliveries".

Like Champagne, revenge is best served cold!

DEALING WITH MULTIPLE MANAGERS

Having more than one manager is tricky. Especially if they do not agree on your focus, what you should do, and the best move for your career and the company. You could end up in a Catch 22 situation where you cannot satisfy one without sacrificing another.

At Ericsson Taiwan, I had six managers – Monica Jansson in Sweden, TY Hsii, local supply division manager, project managers Thomas Jonell and Malcolm de Suza, George Aylmer, project director for the largest client project, and Birger Flygare, the mobile business unit's vice president. The client had their own requirements too, such as customs clearance, site deliveries and the correct allocation of their equipment as it landed in Taiwan.

In Egypt, I had three managers – the project manager, the supply division manager and the client's purchasing department boss.

Building networks in Africa was simpler. I only had two managers to report to; my line manager in Amsterdam and the local Managing Director.

I have often had to report to several managers all with their own priorities and performance targets to meet. All influenced my performance reviews and held the key to my next posting. When your assignment is over, your performance and the needs of local companies decide whether you get a new overseas posting or not.

With the Ericsson network between project and line managers so active, one person's opinion of you can make or break your career.

While I worked for Ericsson, my managers at home had my back. However, as we sourced local material to replace stuff manufactured in Sweden and Europe, we ruffled feathers at the design and engineering department handling product numbering, quality assurance, and site design. We could not justify buying nuts, bolts, cable ladders and cables in Europe, shipping them to a factory in Sweden to be re-labelled with Ericsson product codes, packaged and air shipped to Asia, when we could buy locally manufactured goods. An alliance with the local supply divisions helped us drive through these changes.

Juggling all these aspects was tricky during the Ericsson years as we ran the logistic restructuring only when there was a large GSM network project coming up. The stakes were high, timelines were short, the pressure was on, and too many people wanted to be involved.

When I started my own company, I had only the Board of Directors and shareholders to answer to, but whether you have one or several managers matters not. It's all about how you handle issues as they arise. You and the manager(s) should agree on your tasks and success criteria. Sometimes, having more than one manager can benefit you. You could embark on a dangerous game of chess, playing managers against each other, but that is more likely to slam your career into the ground. Establishing a common goal would be a much wiser course of action. Give your allegiance to the one who can benefit your career the most. Getting plans, instructions, or changes signed off in writing is essential. It could save your skin!

THE QUICK IN AND OUT – OR IS IT?

The administration of short-term contractors is well defined. They are highly task-and-time focused. The contractor is there to quickly solve any problems and get back home to take up the next assignment.

A short-term contractor's role can vary from one assignment to the next. It depends on your skill sets, the current needs, the country you work in, your managers, and if any of your colleagues are there as well. One assignment might be solving a specific problem; the next might be managing a team. Work situations are never static and the assignment scope can change. Ensure your home manager approves any changes as this could affect how your performance is measured.

In order to deliver a first class product to its customers across the globe, Ericsson provided technical experts who flew all over the world to troubleshoot, solve and implement client requests as well as help local organisations build networks.

Running internal improvement projects concurrent with the local subsidiary that is servicing clients with new networks or upgrades, requires a constant and delicate balancing act. We tried running them while there was no actual work, but the changes and the training didn't stick.

So while the local subsidiary was focused on delivering networks against a tight deadline, I had to let the new logistic flow run its course. I had to train and let the local team manage the material deliveries and service the network projects in all aspects. Sometimes I felt as though I was sitting on the fence, but it was the only way to ensure everyone knew what to do and that the project teams gained respect and trust in the new procedures. Initially this created rifts between the network rollout projects and me.

In all projects we ran, we had no real deliverables or line items in a contract to tick off. There was nowhere to send an invoice. When it worked, I flew home. Success was a matter of interpretation.

I created a protective bubble around my teams to help them gain confidence, skills and understanding around their new tasks and processes. Then I let the project teams interface directly with the supply teams, keeping an eye on things but not getting involved. The approached worked in the end, but I set myself up for failure in the short term.

When we started the network rollouts, the projects saw me as an intrinsic part of their team, while my goal was to have the local supply division handle everything themselves within six months. The project and commercial managers thought I should be 100% focused on servicing their project. They could not understand why I was not there for them all the time, why I was not solving problems as they arose, why I was letting the local team do the work or why I sometimes let things crash to highlight the effect of certain actions.

Wise from my experiences with Ericsson, I made a point, when building networks in Africa, of ensuring that everyone in the projects and local companies knew the function of the resources, internal departments, equipment suppliers and consultancy companies. Even with this approach, there were still a few hiccups but we always managed to clear these up before they got out of hand.

When you buy in short-term resources, you need to balance the project's needs with the resource owner's needs. Three issues that can affect this are:

- Insufficient time allocation to solve the problem.

  This could be due to bad planning, unforeseen external dependencies or new additional requirements. The simple solution is to extend the contract but this might not be always possible.

- The resource owner has given the consultant a different scope of work to what was agreed.

  This can be tricky as it raises questions regarding the resource owner's integrity. A frank discussion is usually the best solution.

- Confusion around the rules.

  A specific skillset must follow inherent policies. The resource owner might know what these are, but you, the buyer, might not. Again, an open discussion should solve this.

To achieve a successful short-term assignment, the client, resource owner, and resource must have the same understanding of the tasks, timelines, issues and changes. This sounds basic but many forget to do it.

IMPROVISE, ADAPT, OVERCOME

Apart from cultural and interpersonal problems (more about that later) we had our fair share of technical issues while working with Alcatel to build the Tanzania network for Celtel International. Doesn't matter how well you plan, something will creep up. You just have to deal with it!

Our survey team had missed an entire airport and decided the best place for a 50-meter tower was at the end of the runway!

We misjudged torrential rains and had teams stuck in southwestern Tanzania for a week as the river crossings were too dangerous.

More sinister was a mistake in the equipment specifications with the result that no cell site could communicate with the core network elements. We needed hundreds of converters to get the network working. Alcatel could provide converters but it would take six months and cost a fortune. We had to launch within two weeks. Without the converters, it was not going to happen.

An old colleague who ran Ericsson's office in Tanzania laughed at my problem, saying he had buckets of them lying around in his warehouse. Ericsson could not officially supply Alcatel or Celtel with equipment so they arrived at my office the next day with an invoice from Harry's Mechanical Services. When my boss, Thomas Jonell, asked where I got the converters from, I told him he didn't want to know.

We had several requests from HQ we elected not to follow. They wanted detailed progress updates on work on sites, all sorts of irrelevant stuff I did not want to waste time on. Our project plan for 120 sites and the offices fitted on one A3 sheet and we intended to keep it that way.

I stuck my neck out for my team, trod on toes, broke rules, and delivered the best network build in Africa at that time. We had fun. We respected each other. We shared a common goal and a "get it done!" attitude. Had I failed, my hide would have been stretched from Tanzania to Amsterdam. I could never have done without every single team member. They were the best team I ever had the privilege to lead.

STUPID POLICIES CALL FOR CREATIVITY

In Indonesia, I totalled my Toyota Corolla. A Land Cruiser had run a red light from behind a road construction barricade and Iswar, my driver, had no chance of stopping. There were not even any brake marks. Luckily, something made me use the seatbelt in the back for the first time in three years. Clearly not my time, but it was a close call!

The car was a write-off and my neck hurt from whiplash. Yellow and black bruises from the seat belt crisscrossed my chest. So imagine my fury when some woman from Ericsson Indonesia's HR department told me that my job grading "did not entitle me to seatbelts in the backseat" of my new car, even as I stood there wearing a neck brace. Seriously?

I was fuming, but what could I do?

I had to make a plan! I called Iswar on my mobile.

"Dude," I said, "We need to go to the junk yard."

"Why?"

"We need to remove some seatbelts and put them in the new car." Sorted!

IN SHORT

- Be aware of the different requirements of a local company or project versus the more stable home organisation. Establish a common goal for all managers and team members.

- Get everything – and I mean everything – in writing.

- Seek simple solutions. No solution is so good it cannot be improved and not all mistakes are bad as long as you learn from them.

- Be prepared. Be flexible. Be there.

THE GREAT CULTURAL DIVIDE

"If man is to survive, he will have learned to delight in the essential differences between cultures. Differences in ideas and attitudes are part of life's exciting variety, not something to fear." — Gene Roddenberry

If you think that a Brit with a cell phone and GPS is more sophisticated and better equipped than, say, a Maasai herdsman in Kenya, boy, are you in for a surprise!

So I first discovered on a wreck race from Plymouth in England to Banjul in Gambia when we got lost somewhere in the Mauritanian dessert.

"Right. So where are we? Anyone?" I asked.

"Yeah, I know," said one in our group. He whipped out his brand new GPS.

"Excellent! Show me," I said, wiping off dirt and grease from my hands. We had just jimmied a broken rear suspension arm on our Renault Clio Sport.

"It's just the co-ordinates," he said.

"No problem. We'll plot them on the map," I said. My scout confidence was at its peak. My cocky smile disappeared when we looked at our maps. Not one included coordinates. "Thanks for nothing, Mr Michelin," I thought, tossing the useless maps back into the car.

A guide we had picked up in the last village smiled confidently.

"No need map. I know where. Camp one hour," he said, pointing south somewhere across the desert. He wore a light blue flowing Touareg robe and spoke limited English but appeared composed at all times and drove the cars like a pro.

It was hot. Tempers were short. We had spent the whole day pushing cars, towing cars, digging them out of deep, soft, clinging sand. We got stuck in the sand more often than not. However, it was the guide who saved our bacon. Thanks to him, we found our way back to the camp when our GPS and maps proved to be about as much use as a dead battery.

Our camp was next to a hamlet of three or four huts, where the guide's friends lived. He owned a Toyota Land Cruiser. They had laughed at our cars, so inappropriate for an adventure down the northwest coast of Africa. We dined under the stars, cooking over small fires of camel dung, but that night I awoke with a start.

"Help!"

Was I dreaming or did somebody call out?

"Hey guys. Did you hear that?" I shouted.

"Yeah," answered a muffled voice from a tent nearby. "It's Michael. He's lost."

"Bugger," Nigel growled next to me. "Can someone switch a car on? The lights will lead him back." Having imparted this wisdom, Nigel lay back and was soon snoring again. We shone the headlights and Michael trotted back into camp, wearing a sheepish grin.

"Thanks guys. I needed to pee. Just walked a couple of minutes but then I couldn't see the camp. Everything looks the same in the dark."

Michael had been wandering back and forth, 50 – 100 meters from the camp for more than two hours. All he could see was shrub and dunes in shades of grey. We cracked up.

At the end of the race, we drove down the beach in Senegal, made famous by the Paris-Dakar Rally. Water sprayed off the cars as we raced against the tide. We had to pass a rocky beachhead before it came in. It all went swimmingly until the small Renault Clio with low profile tyres got stuck between submerged rocks. We jumped in the water and lifted it from rock to rock. Mindless of the waist-high water or the car's essential papers under the passenger seat, an Irish lad opened the front door to get a better grip. We scooped out a fish and three offended crabs from the well and dried papers on the bonnet. What a day!

These episodes in the African desert show that without the right tools and techniques we are doomed to fail. When our social tools and techniques are based on ignorance, arrogance, and a lack of awareness, imagine the impact this has on intercultural exchanges.

Here are some of my own examples before we dive into a bit of theory from Professor Geert Hofsteede and Fons Trompenaars.

IT'S THE LITTLE THINGS

"Sorry, Gentlemen, no such person works here." The neat receptionist shrugged.

I looked at my friend. Oops! This could be the shortest summer job ever. We had packed our bags for two months work at Oerlikon-Contraves, a Swiss defence systems manufacturer based in Zurich. The vestibule – filled with life-sized models of the company's products such as satellites, torpedoes, rocket nose cones, missiles, cannons and air surveillance systems – resembled a mad scientist's attic.

We just couldn't get in. The receptionist refused to believe we were to start work there that day. Again, my friend explained who we were looking for.

"Sorry, there's nobody with that name here," she said again.

In thick Swedish-accented German, I tried: "Herrn Ammann?"

Click. Tap. Tap. Click.

"No."

"Urs Ammann?"

More taps on her keyboard.

"No."

A vague memory from my German classes surfaced.

"How about *Herrn Doctor Urs Ammann*?" I ventured.

"Ah. *Herrn Doctor Ammann!*" Her face lit up, she dialled his number from memory, and we were in! Not remembering the importance Germanic cultures put on titles had led to a misunderstanding – my first lesson in small but important cultural differences.

LEAPING OVER LANGUAGE HURDLES

In a multi-national company, you may read an email in Swedish, speak to a colleague in English and hear Swahili spoken by your staff members. Living abroad, you will eventually start thinking and dreaming in a different language.

On business trips, you interact with people who might not speak your language. Most common languages used to be English, French or Spanish. Nowadays, don't be surprised if Chinese or Hindu are the preferred languages.

There will always be nuances in the local dialects that you need to learn. When a South African says he will do something "just now", it means the opposite. It means he will do it at some undetermined future stage when he feels like it, which may or may not happen.

South Africans also say "robot" for traffic light, which can take some getting used to. In Burkina Faso, a South African giving me directions to a location told me to take a right at the second robot. I drove back and forth seeking a mechanical humanoid at the roadside. Had he said "traffic light", I would have been there in 10 minutes!

Within a group of expats, an absurd mix of foreign and local phrases makes for a unique culture and sense of camaraderie. It is a great icebreaker to drop a local phrase in its right context. Drop a *"C'est la vie"* (That is life) into the discussion with French people or a *"Hakuna Matata"* (No problem) in Tanzania. The more effort you make to learn the local language and culture, the more respect you will earn and the easier it is to live in the new country.

When I built mobile networks in Saharan Africa, we discussed concrete, towers, digging, soil, progress and plans in a colourful mix of English, French, Afrikaans, the local language and many signs. We used paper and pen to draw pictures. Our little group created our own language. We all understood each other … well, most of the time.

Understanding languages is a powerful tool. Marjo Baayen, our project planner in Tanzania, spoke fluent Dutch, English and French and understood Swedish. I understood enough Dutch to make our set-up work. The Alcatel team, who supplied the GSM equipment, spoke French and English. They knew I didn't understand enough French to follow their conversations and assumed the same went for Marjo.

During status meetings, the Alcatel team would comment in French to each other about Marjo's great looks or my ignorance. Often they discussed what they should or shouldn't tell us.

At one point, we'd had enough of their crap and Marjo asked me in Dutch if she could give them a piece of her mind. In Swedish,

I told her to go for it. As she gave them a bollocking in fluent French, I rather enjoyed the Alcatel project manager's horrified expression.

From that day onwards, the Alcatel side of the project worked very well.

Marjo and I deliberately masked our language skills to our own business advantage, but sensitivity is also very important. Speaking your own language when others don't understand you cuts them off. Don't do it. How will your local team know it is a social discussion and not about them? The best way to deal with a boss who addresses you in your home language in front of your colleagues or staff who don't speak it, is simply to answer in English. Many times have I had these type of discussions:

"Så, hur går det? Vi har sett raporterna men är allt som det ska?"

"Going OK. We have some delays but nothing we cannot handle."

"Vad menar du? Skapar nån i ditt team problem?"

"No problems. Everything's been working great, the staff are dedicated. We just have some equipment delays."

At the same time, don't just assume people around can't understand your language. I sat in Air France's business class on the way to Ouagadougou, Burkina Faso. Two Swedes sat in front of me discussing their entire negotiation strategy. When leaving the plane, I told them in Swedish that their strategy needed some work! Their expressions were priceless!

Other language traps are abbreviations. The Swedish term for Managing Director is *Verställande Direktör*, abbreviated VD. In English, VD stands for Venereal Disease. When people introduce themselves as Mr Larsson, the VD of ACME Holdings, it can be hard to keep a straight face.

Even harder to get a handle on are the contextual abbreviations. A famous liquor brand launched a campaign in Thailand with the tag line "Absolute 19th". How were they to know that in Thailand, "the 19th" usually referred to the whorehouse after a round of golf?

ONE MAN'S CHORE IS ANOTHER'S REWARD

"Hey Per, check this out," said Mohammed strutting into the office like a peacock.

Glancing up from my laptop, I did a double take. Even though it was sweltering hot outside, Mohammed was dressed for arctic temperatures, wearing new shoes, shirt, coat, leather gloves, a scarf, and even carrying a new briefcase.

"Seriously?" I asked.

"I'm going to Sweden next week," he said.

"I know, but why all the new clothes?"

"It's cold there. And we get a clothing allowance."

Why hadn't I checked out that benefit? I could have used a pair of new surf shorts in Indonesia.

As Mohammed sashayed down the corridor to show off his new threads, I marvelled at how differently local staff viewed business trips to the head office. They saw them as a reward, an incentive. Head office staff, on the other hand, often regarded business trips as a bit of a nuisance – "Why me? What did I do wrong?" – but a necessity. You went, got the job done ASAP, and then flew home – sorted. Next issue?

Mohammed was going to Sweden for training, to meet the project and logistics teams, see the factory, and the other side of the material flow. After that, he was ready to take over the Egypt logistics. That meant my job was done. The processes, systems, and network were up. The warehouse worked. The client was happy. The project logistics unit was back within the supply division where it belonged. Sorted!

WHEN TIME IS RELATIVE

Noon under a sweltering clear blue Sierra Leonean sky but there's no sign of my driver, who is six hours late. When he finally arrives, he's not in the least bit contrite.

Fuming, I ask him what he thought I had meant by 6 o'clock. Turned out that in his culture "6 o'clock" means six hours after sunrise, not six hours after midnight. Riiight.

I had failed to ascertain the difference between Swedish time and local time. It's a common mistake from Northern European expats, especially in Africa. Swedish time dictates an arrival around five minutes earlier than specified. Local time was relative, depending on all sorts of external factors from the traffic to meeting an aunt in the market square.

Foreign business trips are a constant test in cultural navigation skills. Only once you close your hotel room door can you relax. The world is getting smaller and more connected. The work force is more mobile than ever. You can no longer assume that London is British. You cannot learn all Indonesian customs and assume you will be fine in Jakarta. National cultures do not necessarily remain pure within companies – not even if you work for a Swedish company in Sweden. In multicultural environments, assumptions are lethal. We are more aware of other cultures today than before. But, the more culturally skilled we are, the more we can confuse our counterparts by not behaving as expected.

While in Egypt, I received a dinner invitation for 7 pm. Aware of the Egyptians' concept of time especially in the evenings – add on three hours – I rocked up close to 10 pm. How wrong I was! The host, who knew all about the strict Scandinavian adherence to punctuality, had dinner ready by 7.30 pm. In this instance, two rights became one wrong! Our respective cultural knowledge had led to a misunderstanding instead of an enhanced experience.

In Congo DRC, we implemented 'Swedish Time' versus 'Congolese Time' as waiting for people is one of my pet hates. I've learnt over the years that 'Congolese Time' means anything after the agreed time. Even arriving the next day could be acceptable. Why be upset about something you cannot control?

Reconfirming understandings and acknowledging different cultures view on 'time' can eliminate a lot of irritation and time wasting.

BUILDING A CROSS CULTURAL TEAM – FROM COLOURS TO COUNTRIES

I was in Australia finding it hard to suppress my frustration during a meeting contradicting previous agreements about assigned tasks and my reasons for being there.

"Hey Per, stay in blue," said Steve McIntyre, the factory manager.

Excuse me? What the hell did that mean?

Steve explained that "blue" symbolised cool, calm, and constructive attitudes compared with "red" that evoked anger, irritation and non-constructive behaviour. Indeed, certain yoga practises entail inhaling blue for a count of six then exhaling red in a short, sharp burst. Years later, I realised that Steve probably referred to Edward de Bono's lateral thinking concepts, the "6 Thinking Hats".

I looked out over the open-plan office where close to 80 people sat like beehives – installers from Australia and Sweden, a radio planner from the UK, another from Tunisia, and the US, a technical manager and construction guys from Ireland, Swedish testers, academics, and local Indonesians in various functions. Some had formerly built oilrigs in the Gulf. Others were from Ericsson. Such a melting pot of cultures made for an intoxicating mix of opinions in a variety of English accents, all happily working towards the same goal. I did not see any obvious ways our project manager had achieved this but we had created our own subculture. *Vive la différence!*

Allowing all participants to share ideas and experiences is paramount when building cross-cultural teams. Common sense in one culture might be considered madness in another. Overruling without solid agreed foundations can create a dysfunctional team.

When we set up the logistics flow in Taiwan, I had very little experience of intercultural management. I only knew that to get the project going, I needed total buy-in from all links in the supply chain and for everyone to understand the scope and their individual roles.

I needed people from the engineering department, customer project managers, external suppliers, commercial people, shipping people, Taiwan customs officials, the warehousing team and logisticians on the same page. To get all these people into one room was impossible.

Instead, we created "black boxes" for various functions, grouped them and work-shopped with each group, focusing on input requirements and output data. Tasks changed as we found loose ends. Once done with the first draft mapping, all people partook in a dry run of the whole process. Each unit had to explain what and how they did things and what the output meant.

The "black box" mapping, definition of outputs, the dry run in Taiwan and overall understanding of each link's role created a sense of purpose for all. We had created our own culture with Swedish, Taiwanese, and Australian influences.

We had also put faces to names and e-mails, often the hardest part to achieve. There are countless examples where hierarchical communication channels hinder the daily work progress. Meeting each other, discussing goals and understanding each other's situations made for communication that is more effective.

Ericsson Egypt was my fifth supply-chain restructuring project. I interfaced with management levels I would not have access to in Sweden, discussed issues directly with the client's management and we took immediate decisions.

The different attitudes towards work between home organisation and project culture still amazes me. In the projects, it was all about delivery and getting it done! Not "how" or "who", but "when" – with rewards based on delivery. You got a new assignment if you proved you could deliver. Back home it was about processes. About how things were done and who might authorise actions.

A rather sad part was the difference in attitude towards local staff and expats. Much of my freedom in decision-making and access to management levels stemmed from being an expat. Local staff had to fit into the local hierarchy and local authorisation levels.

In Tanzania, the project team was in disarray. There was no focus or common goal. Everyone just did what he thought best. The subcontractors were being paid a daily rate just to sit around.

On top of this, the approved budget only catered for two thirds of the costs and there were no plans in place. The project team comprised 14 core staff – a couple of Tanzanians, a New Zealander, some South Africans, and a few Indians. The company CEO was a Brit, the CFO a Malawian, the COO was South African, two HR consultants were from UK and the architect was from Gabon. Several high-level managers flew in from Holland every now and again. Add to this mix, a Swede, two Brits, a Pilipino, a Frenchman, an Azerbaijan and chaos prevailed.

Based on my Taiwanese experience and four network projects for Celtel in Africa, I pulled the handbrake on all activities. While the technical experts re-planned the network, I sent the subcontractors home. I was not the most popular guy in town.

We needed to firm up the project and the various units' tasks. This time we let all units do their own "black box" mapping. I talked about how the reactions of different cultures to the same situations, using Professor Hofstede's graphs. After two days, phrases like "Don't be so bloody Swedish!" or "You are getting very African on me!" abounded along with jokes about the French and their long lunches, the African concept of time and the Swedish way of wanting things done immediately.

The new technical plans for the network slotted into a well-defined process where everyone knew what to do. We had created another unique project culture by mixing people, nationalities and tasks into one unified whole. Within two months, this amazing team had launched Celtel's mobile services in Dar es Salaam.

When everyone has the same goal, project members become ambassadors for implemented changes, irrespective of culture or nationality. Nothing proves the point better, than achieving the goals.

The 'blue' and 'red' discussion in Australia had been useful but instead of colours, I used countries. The most valuable result was that differences became fun. It created a unique project culture where we all belonged.

THE SWEDE ABROAD AND AT HOME

Let's face it. We Swedes are an odd bunch. Hard working, outdoorsy, tall blonde Viking stereotypes that walk or cycle everywhere. Many Swedes are social (on their own terms) but – it must be said – can be a tad boring and reserved.

Foreign visitors who witness the Swedish 4.20 pm office exodus are amazed. One minute it's a hive of activity, the next minute the empty offices are quiet as a tomb.

Swedes make a rigid distinction between work – eight hours in the office – and private time. Family and friends are important to them, as are constant coffee breaks.

My sister is a perfect example. Some 12 years back, she started a new job and got a work cell phone. This was great as I battled to get hold of her while working and travelling in Africa. Getting through was impossible, especially after hours. One day I asked her why. Her answer stunned me: "It is a work phone; I switch it off when I leave the office."

I pointed out that it was a mobile phone and you could have it on and screen calls but she was having none of it. Such a typical Swedish attitudes frustrates the heck out of someone like me, who never switches off my phone.

Colleagues at the local offices would never let you sit in the hotel alone on a Friday night. They love to show you a good time in their city. As a Swede abroad, I was always touched by the hospitality extended to me by foreigners. People constantly invited me for a drink, or even dinner at their home. Sadly, Swedes seldom extend the same courtesy to foreigners in Sweden, though it must be said that in the foreign countries, the Swedish expats epitomise bonhomie. It's as if our values change and we become different people when we leave Sweden. Work and private life now merges into a richer blend. Socialising after work is accepted.

Might it be because the expatriate couple has more time available? Back home in Sweden most couples juggle two jobs, kids, housework, and social activities. Out on contract it is usually only one person working and there's invariably a house cleaner, gardener, and driver to help with chores. No need to do washing or all the other small simple things that take time and energy from a working couple in Sweden. Away from the motherland, the houses are always tidy and ready for guests. We have time for each other and we take the time. Whatever the reasons are, it is an interesting side effect of expat life.

THE THREE POWER PYRAMIDS

"Ah, how lovely to see the sisters together again," said our chairman with a cunning smile, looking straight at me.

What? I looked closer at the two women and cringed. They were real sisters. Oops!

I had been trying for months to get one of them fired for utter incompetence – protecting and putting non-performing staff ahead of company goals, just for starters. Seeing her with her sister – the company secretary – made me understand why she still had a job. Nepotism.

I filed that information for future use. We exchanged pleasantries waiting for the meeting to start, as if nothing happened. However, I had received the message, loud and clear!

We seldom discuss the informal hierarchies found in multinational subsidiaries. These hierarchies flourish outside the organisation chart. I have found there are three different hierarchies in most companies: The official, the local, and the expatriate.

The official power pyramid follows the company's organisation chart. The CEO is the boss with his departmental managers below him. Formal decision-making follows the prescribed authority levels.

Being subtle, the local power pyramid is harder to identify in the beginning. You need to look at who goes to lunch with whom, who plays golf with whom, who is involved in meetings outside his job scope, who gets stuff done, and who is highly rated by the expatriate power pyramid? You need to look at family relationships. Who goes to which social functions outside of work? Finding out this information takes time and ingenuity. The more accepted and respected you are, the easier it will be to map it out.

Expatriates populate their own power pyramid, where cultural acceptance is not as important as the closeness of said expat and his family to the ambassador and if he has worked with the expat boss before. How important for the subsidiary is the expat's current project? How big a budget does he control? How long has he been working for the company? Is he famous in expat circles? What is his golf handicap? Club memberships and reputation among the local staff also play an important part.

The three power pyramids coexist within the same company – an unbeatable force when they work in harmony but the opposite is true if they work against each other.

Local hierarchy players think about the long term. They care about the company and the local community's perception of them. Conversely, the expatriate hierarchy, being short term, focuses on personal gains and having a great time. Within two to three years, expats move on to the next assignment. The local hierarchy players know that in 10 years' time, they will still be there, while the expatriates have come and gone.

When I took over as project director for Tanzania, the project had been running for more than five months but not one site lease had been signed. We had no real estate to build on. People just milled around wasting time and money. I restructured the project and gave Stephano, the local site acquisition manager, additional responsibilities. I gave him the freedom and authority to perform his tasks. Suddenly the signed and approved sites started rolling in.

Within a month, we had enough to start the construction phase of the project. Nobody had liked the previous project director, and the local hierarchy had worked against him. Stephano was high up in the local power pyramid and by empowering him; the two hierarchies started aligning and working for the same goal. We started getting stuff done.

HOW TO IDENTIFY CULTURAL DIFFERENCES

Identifying cultural differences is hard but there are a few tricks such as keeping abreast of the local media. What newspapers write about and TV anchors discuss is important for the local population.

Look at adverts. What is the message being conveyed? What are the aspirations and the beauty ideals? What brands are spending on advertising? What sports are the people watching and playing? Is it a soccer or rugby nation? Are there social differences between soccer fans and cricket fans? Are people watching sports in stadiums or in the pub? Do sports interests differ between cities?

Observe people in detail. How are they dressed? How do they greet each other? What do they drink in cafés? Do they go to markets or shopping malls? When do they come in and when do they leave the office? Do they use cars, bikes or public transport? And so on.

Understand the climate. Are there seasons? Are winters or rainy months cold or warm? Is the country in the southern or northern hemisphere? Do they have typhoons or a hot dessert wind?

Read about the country's history. Visit some of the historical sites. Not only is it educational, you show respect for your host country and most of it is interesting.

At local restaurants look at what the locals eat and how they order? Do they select from the menu or argue with the chef? How about religions? Do people go to church on Sundays, the mosque on Fridays, or attend Schul on Friday nights? Are state and religion separate?

What about attitudes towards the government? Do people respect their government officials? Do they participate in elections? Is the country democratic or secular?

Read up on the economy. What is the main produce and export? What are the industrial centres? Imports? Aid? Are there specific agricultural areas? What do they grow? What about forex? Does the country's economy rise and ebb with oil prices?

Compare your observations with your own culture and previous countries you've lived in. Update them with new experiences and reflections to build your own cultural chart.

PROFESSOR GEERT HOFSTEDE'S AND FONS TROMPENAARS' WORKS

A university course about Intercultural Management exposed me to Professor Geert Hofstede's theories and findings relating to Cultural Dimensions: Power Distance, Uncertainty Avoidance, Individualism versus Collectivism, Masculinity versus Femininity, Long-Term Orientation and Indulgence versus Restraint.

Professor Hofstede originally used employee values scores collected by IBM between 1967 and 1973 in 70 countries as a basis. Resent research and new employee value scores indicate that there has been little change in the last 40 years. Identified culture dimensions are national culture differences and not organisational cultures. The latter differs in the use of symbols, heroes and rituals while the national culture goes to the core values of a nation.

So what are these cultural dimensions? According to the definitions in Cultures and Organisations, Software of the Mind, they are:

Power Distance:

Power Distance is the extent to which the less powerful members of organisations and institutions (like the family) accept and expect that power is distributed unequally. This represents inequality (more versus less), but defined from below, not from above. It suggests that followers endorse a society's level of inequality as much as the leaders. Power and inequality, of course, are fundamental facts of any society and anybody with international experience will be aware that 'all societies are unequal, but some are more unequal than others'.

Uncertainty Avoidance:

The Uncertainty Avoidance dimension deals with a society's tolerance for uncertainty and ambiguity. It indicates to what extent a culture programmes its members to feel uncomfortable or comfortable in unstructured situations. Unstructured situations are novel, unknown, surprising, and different.

Uncertainty-avoiding cultures try to minimize the possibility of such situations by strict laws and rules, safety and security measures, and on the philosophical and religious level by a belief in absolute Truth: "there can only be one Truth and we have it". People in uncertainty-avoiding countries are also more emotional, and motivated by inner nervous energy. The opposite type, uncertainty-accepting cultures, are more tolerant of different opinions; try to have as few rules as possible, and on the philosophical and religious level they are relativistic and allow many currents to flow side by side. People within these cultures are more phlegmatic and contemplative, and not expected by their environment to express emotions.

Individualism:

Individualism on the one side versus its opposite –
collectivism – is the degree to which individuals are integrated into
groups. On the individualist side, we find societies in which the ties
between individuals are loose and everyone is expected to look after
themselves and their immediate family. On the collectivist side, we
find societies in which people from birth onwards are integrated into
strong, cohesive extended families (with uncles, aunts and
grandparents) that protect them in exchange for unquestioning
loyalty. The word collectivism in this sense has no political meaning:
it refers to the group, not the state.

Masculinity versus Femininity:

Masculinity versus Femininity refers to the distribution of
emotional roles between the genders – another fundamental issue for
any society. IBM studies revealed that (a) women's values differed
less among societies than men's values; (b) men's values from one
country to another ranged from very assertive and competitive on the
one hand to modest and caring – similar to women's values – on the
other.

Long-Term Orientation:

Long-term oriented societies foster virtues slanted towards future rewards, in particular saving, persistence, and adapting to changing circumstances. Short-term oriented societies foster virtues related to the past and present such as national pride, respect for tradition, preservation of "face", and fulfilling social obligations.

Indulgence versus Restraint:

An indulgent society allows gratification of natural human drives related to enjoying life and having fun. A restrained society suppresses and regulates gratification of needs by means of strict social norms.

Dimension scores are relative:

The country scores on these dimensions are relative - societies are compared to other societies. These relative scores have proven to be stable over decades. The forces that cause cultures to shift tend to be global or continent-wide - they affect many countries at the same time, so that if their cultures shift, they shift together, and their relative positions remain the same.

This last point Professor Hofstede stresses is important. The cultural dimensions and scoring within one dimension are relative. They do not mean anything as a standalone value. Comparing two groups and their relative difference shows where you are and where you are going.

In *Riding the Waves of Culture, Understanding Diversity in Global Business*, Fons Trompenaars, Charles Hampden-Turner and Peter Woolliams look at seven ways of classifying cultural dimensions:

Universalism versus Particularism:

Does a society puts greater value on the obligations of relationships or on the individual?

Individualism versus Communitarianism:

This is how various cultures value the individual and the community.

Neutral versus Emotional:

This measures the importance and acceptance of showing emotions.

Specific versus Diffuse:

This looks at the value of relationships based on human contact versus contractual relationships.

Achievement versus Ascription:

Here the authors look at how value to the individual is set. Is it by achievements, records, connections, gender, schools attended or age?

Attitudes to Time:

Different cultures see time differently. Does it move in a straight line where all things happen sequentially or does past mix with present and future?

Attitudes to the Environment:

This dimension is less about climate change and more about how you perceive people around you. Are you looking from inside out or outside in when deciding on an action? Are you looking at the effect on yourself or the effect on others?

Irrespective of which dimension system is used, all cultures vary. Discussions about cultural differences can be theoretical and abstract. To show the cultural differences, I used a couple of Professor Hofstede's cultural dimension values. The plots below are selected for their visual values. I have circled the Scandinavian countries and groups of countries I have worked in. Nothing is definite, but the graphs below illustrate how intercultural differences can be used as a baseline.

Picture 1: Power Distance vs. Individualism/Collectivism

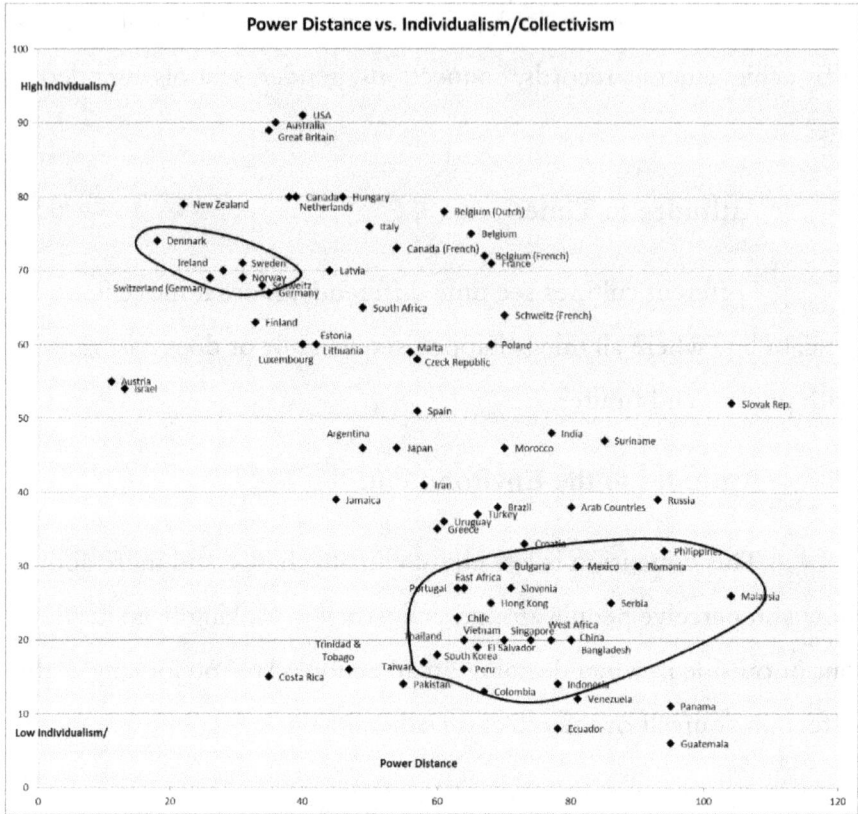

Power Distance vs. Individualism/Collectivism

In picture 1, the relative distance between the Scandinavian countries and East Asian and African countries is quite large.

Picture 2: Power Distance vs. Uncertainty Avoidance

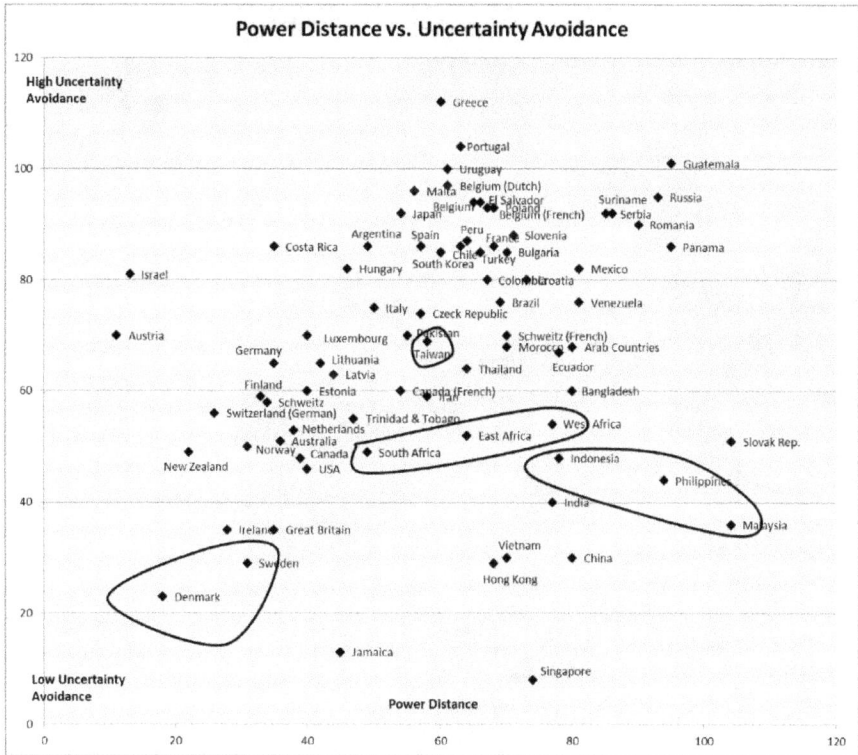

Power Distance vs. Uncertainty Avoidance

In picture 2, we can see that the African countries have a difference in Power Distance, but are similar in respect of Uncertainty Avoidance. Note Taiwan, which was close to the South East Asian countries in regards to Individualism, differs with regards to Uncertainty Avoidance. This implies that we cannot generalise countries in a region based on only one or two dimensions.

Picture 3: Power Distance vs. Masculinity/Femininity

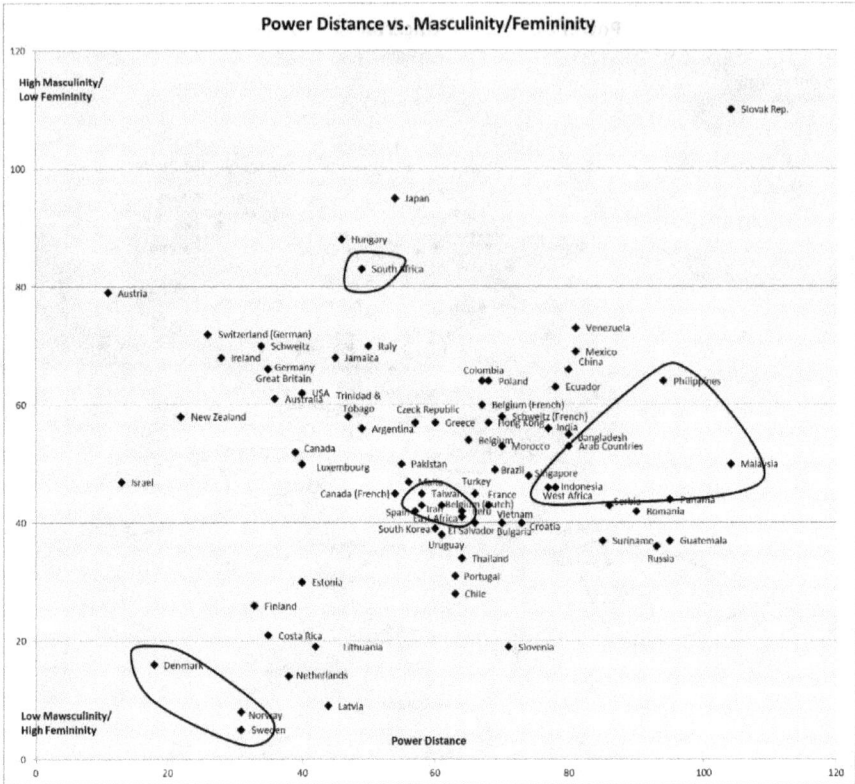

In picture 3, Taiwan and the South East African countries are similar in Masculinity. Note South Africa's distance to East Africa and West Africa within this dimension.

Picture 4: Long-Term Orientation vs. Indulgence/Restraint

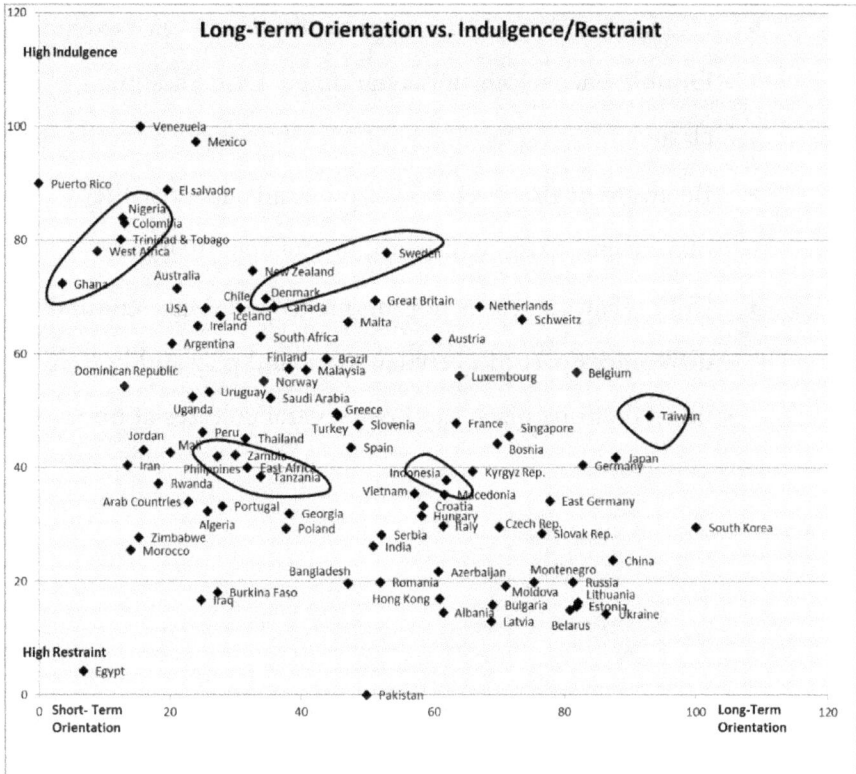

Long-Term Orientation vs. Indulgence/Restraint

In picture 4, Sweden and Indonesia are similar concerning Long-Term Orientation but different with regards to Indulgence.

The graphs show there will always be cultural minefields. Occasionally you'll step on a landmine but if you're prepared, this need not sound the death knell for your project. Awareness of cultural subtlety is the way forward.

IN SHORT

- Use language to communicate and include - not exclude. Double-check your understandings. Don't assume - clarify!
- Be aware of the three power pyramids, identify the players and work with them, not against them.
- Cultural awareness is not unique to you. Make cultural differences part of everyday work and play and keep in mind that one place can host several cultures at once.

THE OTHER SIDE OF EXPAT LIFE

"You're an expatriate. You've lost touch with the soil. You get precious.
Fake European standards have ruined you. You drink yourself to death.
You become obsessed with sex. You spend all your time talking, not
working. You are an expatriate, see? You hang around cafes." –
Ernest Hemingway, The Sun Also Rises

Sometimes you just need to jump out of the nest and learn to fly on the way down. Standing in the check-in queue at Sweden's Arlanda airport in September 1997 I felt nervous and excited. All I needed for a year in Indonesia weighed less than 20 kg. My rented 30 m² apartment had been packed up in less than four hours – 31 years of stuff in a storage company outside Stockholm.

Little did I know another 15 years would roll by before I'd see my stuff again. For now, my entire life was in my suitcase. What would the expat journey bring me? I was young, naïve and eager to discover. Here's what I learnt.

THERE'S NO PLACE LIKE HOME

Spend too much time in foreign countries and you start to feel like a stranger in your own land. As I snuggled into my tourist class seat, arranged the pillow, wrapped the thin, static blanket around myself and made inroads into my second bottle of wine, I smiled.

After seven months in Taipei, I was on my way home and couldn't wait to share all my exotic experiences with my Swedish friends and colleagues.

The first thing that struck me as I walked into the office was how unhurried everyone was – no frantic outbursts, no running, nobody working around the clock. The day started with a cup of coffee and some chitchat about the summer vacations in Sweden. The excitement of being back to tell everyone about amazing Taiwan, wore off fast. Nobody wanted in-depth details. They wanted to discuss weekend plans and where to have beers later.

Then you notice you're drifting away from certain friends. Conversations feel foreign when you don't care who broke up with whom or what the prime minister is about to announce, because your next flight is in three days. As friends become fewer, your sense of home begins to dissipate.

On the plus side, you discover your real friends. I'm lucky enough to have some in Sweden. After dinner with them, I can fall asleep on their sofa, and will awaken the next morning to find a blanket over me and their Rhodesian Ridgeback snuggling up. True friends. Forever.

Distance and the cost of travelling create problems, especially when you spend more time in the air than with your kith and kin. Friendships are two-way streets and require nurturing and presence. When my two-week assignment in Indonesia got extended to three months, I was about to miss a good friend's wedding in Sweden. Instead I flew from Jakarta on a Friday afternoon, landed in Stockholm on Saturday morning, worked a few hours, took a taxi to the wedding, partied all night, took a taxi back to the office, worked some more, then took another taxi to the airport to be back in Jakarta by Monday evening. Was I knackered or what! Still, it was a great party and worth every minute of the flight.

Today, thanks to Skype, social media, and apps that allow you to communicate with anyone in the world cheaply, astronomical phone bills are no longer an excuse not to maintain contact.

So, Expat, phone home!

WHEREVER YOU LAY YOUR HAT ...

"Welcome back, Mr Ostberg."

The little word 'back' makes all the difference. 'Back' implies that you're not just another guest. You are a regular – something most business travellers aim for. If you are alone, it feels homey. If you are with other people, you imagine their respect.

The 5-star hotels you prefer are associated with your frequent flyer program and paid for by the company. You get fluffy clean towels every day, access to gym and saunas. You never have to make your bed. You eat out as often as you wish, enjoying a nice bottle of wine or a drink at the bar after work – all paid by your company travel allowance.

You may spot famous actors across the lobby or relax in the sauna after work. Sounds great, right? And it can be – provided your company treats you fairly and you don't fall into one of the many traps awaiting the unsuspecting expat.

BOOZE, BOOZE, AND MORE BOOZE

Tuesday, noon: I look down at my ringing phone. My Swedish friend Benny is calling.

"Tjenna Benny. Hur är läget?" I ask. Benny and I had been on a bender in Jakarta's city centre a few nights back. The last I saw of him he was climbing into his car with a new girl.

"Hello?" comes the answer in English with an Indonesian accent. "Do you know the owner of this phone?"

Say, what? Had something happened to Benny?

"Yes," I answer. "What's up?"

"Good! We need your help here".

"Where is Benny?"

"Who? I am bartender at Hard Rock Café. The owner of this phone is lying on floor. Can you come, please?"

Half an hour later, as we carried Benny out from Hard Rock, the bartender explained that Benny had shown up a few hours earlier. He had fallen off his barstool during his umpteenth Long Island cocktail. The booze had knocked him out cold.

When he woke up the next day, Benny and I had a chat. He was lonely and had few real friends, a common situation for single guys. We all worked and played hard. Benny was far from the only colleague I had to carry home from dodgy nightspots in Jakarta or Manila.

Hard partying isn't the worst thing. Social drinking can just as easily push you into alcoholism. One of my managers in Africa would down a two-fingered whiskey tot before work every morning. In the Philippines after finishing a project, I finally tracked down the local project sponsor to a seedy strip bar where he'd been for three days straight. Reeking of sweat and alcohol, he was still drunk as a skunk.

Take a lonely night at the hotel, an eight-hour layover, or a free afternoon at the pool and you can see how easy it is for expats to fall into the alcohol trap. Why not order another G&T or a second bottle of wine for dinner? You're worth it, right? You had a good day.

If the lonely nights don't get you, the social scene encourages more drinking – pre and post-prandial snifters with friends, a few beers after golf or squash, receptions, functions, it never stops. Soon, you can barely function without a glass of wine at lunch to take the edge off.

Drinking allows us to reveal our true selves behind the social facades. Drinking is part of the group initiation in many cultures, a way to get to know each other. Amazingly, it is socially accepted in business meetings and discussions to have a glass of wine or a whiskey before, during and after. A Swedish diplomat in South Korea once told me it was better to be able to "handle lots of alcohol than be too restrained".

One Ericsson colleague had to quit her sales job and find another position because all the business required drinking with clients was turning her into an alcoholic. She's happy she had the strength to climb off the wagon before things spiralled out of control.

In my experience, companies do not care for expat staff with alcohol problems. Neither do they take responsibility for finding them professional help. They rather give the functioning alcoholic good references and transfer him from one country to another. Everyone just passes the buck.

It went against my own ambitious Swedish mind-set but after some years in East Asia, I came to agree with the old diplomat. Raise a glass or three, as long as you know when to get out.

SEX, DRUGS, ROCK 'N' ROLL

"4 am – if I'm ever up that early, it's because I'm up that late." — Jarod Kintz, This Book Has No Title

Bodies pack the small dance floor under pulsating strobe lights and pumping music. Ten G&T's down and I'm making like John Travolta in *Grease*. My driver taps my shoulder.

"Mr Per, we need to go now!" he shouts into my ear.

"Why? The party just started."

"If we leave now, you have time to shower and change before your 7.30 am meeting. It's 6 am."

"Already? Shit!"

Life on a short-term assignment can feel like one long speed-dating excursion. For the group of singles that travelled around Asia for Ericsson, time sped by in a blur of work, dinners, parties, and nightclubs.

We'd leave work at 11 pm, meet the gang at a restaurant, party until dawn – grabbing an hour's shut-eye and a Red Bull – before hitting the office again. Seven days a week! The first real sleep we got was on the flight home.

It starts when you arrive. You slide into the back of a limo that whisks you off to your hotel. You check in, meet some colleagues in the bar for a quick drink and chat, and get driven to the office the next morning. It's a surreal world.

Local happenings are of little importance when you're leaving soon. You tend to gravitate to short-term colleagues or find a young, irresponsible party crowd to hang with. Of course, there are also the local girls. Some guys hook up with a girl for the duration; others change partners every night, breathing new meaning into the word short-term.

The more stable folk have been in the country longer or are there with family. They keep to themselves. The people you meet are not your real friends. Like you, they are there for work. One of the most common questions is "How long are you here for?" It can feel deliciously intoxicating or you may find yourself sitting in the bar feeling lonely in a crowd and wondering when your life suddenly became so empty.

Apart from alcohol, there's easy access to all kinds of drugs – Ecstasy, LSD, cocaine, weed, whatever you want. The nightclubs are full of it. Your newfound friends will say: "Loosen up, man. It's just a few lines."

You have to be strong if you are to avoid being swept up in it all. Look, I'm no saint – don't get me wrong. In Indonesia, I partied all night, every night, and lived on energy drinks for weeks. I lost 5kg in two months. I've smoked joints from rooftops in Cairo and in Saigon's street cafes. I spent four days at Koh Phangan's Full Moon Party high as a kite, carried a kilo of weed through Vietnam and tried to smoke as much of it as possible in five weeks. I got away with it. I was lucky, but luck is not something you want to rely on. Don't take stupid risks. Rather hang onto your values and sanity. You're worth it.

LONELINESS

You see him all over the world in hotel restaurants, bars, and airport lounges – the lone traveller dragging a carry-on, working on a laptop, reading a newspaper. Mostly he's a 'he'. Often, it's me.

Few bother to ask another single person to share a meal and have a chat. You risk being intrusive. He might think you are trying to pick him up so you remain in your own world.

Social media has made things a little easier. You can connect with family and friends like the businessman I saw having dinner with his family via Skype. He was at the Hilton hotel in Johannesburg. They were in Europe, but their conversation sounded heartfelt and meaningful.

Other businessmen, however, buy some company to share those lonely nights with …

THE ILLICIT BUSINESS BONK

Many of my colleagues – single and married – consider picking up hookers at a strip bar after work perfectly normal, just because they're in a foreign country.

Why do so many of us shed our morals so easily when we're abroad? I have seen hard-core South African white supremacists sampling the local flavour the day they hit a new African country and

Swedes leaving conferences early for a quick bite before hitting the girlie bars. In East Asia, one manager's wife caught him screwing the maid downstairs while he thought his wife was in the shower upstairs. A contractor in Tanzania got such a bad reputation for picking up a new girl every night that I had to send him home.

I have seen teary farewells between European women and local beach boys at Banjul airport in Gambia, the boys already checking out the new arrivals over the women's shoulders.

One day when coming home to our company guesthouse, I found a middle-aged European woman on our veranda, waiting with a suitcase next to her. After a little chitchat, I realised she was the wife of one of my consultants, who had taken up with a local girl. This will be fun, I thought. Fortunately for him I was able to call and warn him from my room.

In Sierra Leone, the UN forces, British Army and Red Cross freely availed themselves of the hookers. Particularly ironic when the Red Cross staff taught local Sierra Leoneans about HIV/AIDS and the risks of a promiscuous life during the days.

Client meetings are booked in strip bars. Contracts signed on the butts of naked girls. Business associates and politicians come with their own full "service" staff with "happy endings" all round.

Many hotels allow prostitutes to solicit business in the bar and pool areas. At one hotel in Dar es Salaam, the hookers at the bar outnumbered the guests. The hotel's reputation and popularity went downhill fast.

When you sit alone at a hotel or in a bar in Africa, the local girls will accost you no matter how often you say a polite 'no thanks'. At one bar when I wanted to drink my beer and watch a soccer game, a girl and her pimp started a fight with me simply because I was not interested in her services.

What you see, hear, and experience, can challenge your morals. Bars and nightclubs throb with girls who will declare their eternal love to you. You may see undesirable sides of your colleagues but you need to work with them on a daily basis, irrespective of their choices.

I am not judging, just pointing out the facts. Only you can decide for yourself how far you are prepared to stretch your own values before you become jaded and cynical.

MOMENTARY MELTDOWNS

It is pitch-dark. You are drenched in a cold sweat in a hotel room, sheets tangled around you. You cannot move. Your heart is pounding. You have no idea where you are. You fumble for the light, managing to locate the stationary you threw off the night table to make space for the laptop and books.

"Hotel Memling, Kinshasa, Democratic Republic of Congo" it says. Riiight! And, you're here because …? Fumbling around, the calendar eventually shows a couple of meetings with the mobile operators and dinner with the local lawyer. Ok. You can go back to sleep.

Laugh if you like, but that has happened to me a few times and it's scary as hell. Disorientation can creep up and smack you when you least expect it. One of my friends called his wife in the middle of the night to ask her where he was. She was not impressed.

These mini meltdowns can happen to the best of us. At Heathrow airport, Jon Steele, a British ITN cameraman, suddenly had no idea who he was or where he was going. He later wrote 'War Junkie' (published by Transworld), an excellent book about his experiences that took him to some of the world's toughest areas.

FORGETTING TO EXPLORE THE COUNTRY

The work and party hard ethos is a trap until you smell the coffee and start using your weekends off for sightseeing and learning more about your host country.

In my case, focusing on the job meant that for the first two years with Ericsson, I saw little of the places I went to. I flew on weekends. I worked and partied hard, sleeping on the flights between Asia and Sweden.

The Swedish union's overtime rules changed the game for me. Within three months, I had exhausted the year's overtime allocation. I didn't care. I was having fun, living my dream. I enjoyed the work and didn't see why the union's rules should stop me.

However, I was burning the candle in both ends. My manager and I found a way to offset the excessive accumulated overtime. It worked out. I started to see and experience more of the countries I visited for work. The trips got longer but I enjoyed them more. When I did this, I began to feel far more at ease. I saw nuances I had missed before. I found balance in my life.

Arranging vacations within your business trips really is a healthier way for all, especially the families. Who cares if the taxman doesn't like it?

FAMILY DYNAMICS

Visiting and working in a foreign country are vastly different. Once you're a resident, cultural differences crop up and financial reality bites. Mundane everyday tasks replace the dream of paradise. You get tired of answering the same questions from envious tourists. How did you end up here? What is there to do? How do I get a permit to open a bar? How can I buy a place?

In Borneo, after months of answering the same questions from backpackers, I withdrew from the social scene. I busied myself helping villagers taste their rice wine and took hikes in the jungle. I was able to do more or less as I pleased because I was single.

When you travel, time is relative. For you it's a short week cramming in four to six consultations a day, meeting people, and eating out every night, but for the people left at home having to take care of everything, your week away can feel like a month.

You miss your daughter's first date and your son's goal for the soccer team. Your wife's upset because you didn't come home when you said you would. Of course, it's hard to stick to arrangements when you never know how long you will really be away.

One two-week stint in Jakarta, Indonesia, stretched into a three-month stay for me, due to unexpected challenges. I had to stay on, run the logistics, and train the local team.

If you take your family overseas with you, it is important for your own wellbeing that they feel at home. Few spouses get work permits in the new country and making new adjustments can affect family dynamics, and strain relationships. Also, some expats discover they have hopelessly under budgeted. The cool beach hut does not work for small kids. Or they have to pay for schooling – something they forgot to factor in – and now cannot afford visits to family and friends back home.

Setting out the benefits for its expatriates is a delicate balance of costs for many companies. Some focuses on the financial package, others on the softer aspects of helping make the transition as smooth as possible for their employees. Having heard many complaints, I guess we expats will never be happy.

If you have a family back home, you will need to fit into their groove on your return. It takes work. Keeping friendships is also difficult. All your friends are finding partners and getting married while you're still footloose and fiancé free.

Short-term jobs abroad can mean a couple of months to a year, or longer, away from your loved ones. Not every relationship can handle that. Yes, I was single most of the time I travelled for

Ericsson and Celtel and all my travelling ensured I remained single. I once arrived two hours late for a dinner date. This was before everyone in Sweden had mobile phones. Amazingly, my date was still there. I told her I had to go back to the office after dinner and that I was flying to Australia the next day. She stood up and left. I never saw her again.

IN SHORT

- You won't grow if you stay in the expat bubble, so get out more, mingle with the locals, and explore your host country.

- Familiarise yourself with the local policies and prices prior to moving to another country. Ask friends and colleagues, who live there for advice.

- Try not to fall into the party trap but at least know when to climb out if you do. Listen to your friends' comments; they are truer than you think.

- Maintain the friendships you care about and keep in touch with your family. With today's technology making it so easy, there are no excuses.

COMING HOME

"Safe trip home, wherever home is. I hope you find it." – A village chief's daughter said this to me in Borneo in 1993

We all know how the princess kissed the frog to turn him into a handsome prince. Well, the reverse can happen when you come home from your overseas posting. Gone are the servants, mansion, swimming pool, free golf club memberships, driver and free car. You've become just another middle manager in the company. In short, you're a frog!

Having worked in 11 Asian and African countries, by 36 my work perks included cars equipped with a driver, houses – most with pool, maid and gardener, all a far cry from my rented 30 m^2 apartment in Stockholm.

Few companies offer a "homecoming reintegration" even though statistics show that the longer you stay away from home, the harder it is to reintegrate again. This is one of the reasons many companies try to bring their expatriates home every two or three years, before sending them out on a new posting.

It is also common to hit a depression when coming home from an assignment. You go from high-octane work to tedium. To reintegrate, you need to treat home as a new place and assume you know nothing. Learn to be Swedish (if you're Swedish) again. Take the time to reconnect. Don't expect re-integration support from the company but if you're lucky enough to be offered – take it! You have to rebuild relationships at home and in the workplace yourself.

Back home, everything has changed, including you. You're no longer the big deal you were in the host country with all its perks. Now there are other reality checks to face such as the housework – laundry, vacuuming, fetching kids, public transport to work, and so on.

If you bring home a partner you met while away, things can get complicated. Back there, you lived in luxury, now you don't. Often there's a language issue. When you met, English, French or Spanish were the languages spoken, but not everyone speaks those back home. Your partner can feel isolated.

In Sweden and many other countries, you are both expected to work. If your spouse cannot speak Swedish, it is hard to get a job, even with a work permit. It took more than 10 years for an Indonesian girl who married one of my colleagues to get Swedish citizenship. They had to go for couples' interviews every six months. Each partner is questioned separately with the answers compared afterwards. Intrusive questions like 'how many times do you have sex every week?' and 'What does your spouse like to do in bed?' The Spanish Inquisition sounds more fun!

Even though my South African girlfriend and I have lived together more than 10 years, she still gets the third degree every time she applies for just a tourist visa to Sweden.

Having lived abroad for more than 18 years, home – for me – is where the heart is.

IN SHORT

- Prepare for coming home as diligently as you prepared for leaving. Maintain your connection to home as much as you can while you are away.
- Things change, so treat your homecoming like a move to a new country again.
- Do not take things for granted just because it is 'home'.

DOING BUSINESS IN AFRICA

"No other continent has endured such an unspeakably bizarre combination of foreign thievery and foreign goodwill." — Barbara Kingsolver, The Poisonwood Bible

SIMPLY UNINSURABLE!

Life changing decisions can be scary. Sitting in Heathrow's departure lounge, waiting to meet one of Celtel International's Project Directors to help me get started in Sierra Leone, my mind filled with doubts. Had I done the right thing? What would it be like to work for a Dutch company in Africa?

Working as a Project Director for a mobile operator was a few rungs further up the career ladder. On the phone, Thomas Jonell had said it would be easy. "Just build some towers, install some equipment, do some testing, *voilà!* Done!" Yeah, right.

"Oh, I almost forgot. You need to open a company. We cannot pay individuals; your company must invoice us," he added.

Sierra Leone would be my first project. Flights were booked. I had four weeks to open a company – and over the festive season to boot. Thomas' casual request had sent me even further into the unknown.

Now that I was a self-employed consultant, I had to handle all the admin that Ericsson had previously taken care of – medical and life insurances, phones, laptop, travel cash.

When I called to sort out my life and medical insurance and listed the countries I might work in, the sales rep started laughing. Yes, I knew about blood diamonds, I told her. Yes, and the 'one hand – one vote' policy. How about the exploitation of Nigeria by oil companies? Yip, that hardly came as a surprise. Yes, I knew all about African diseases such as Ebola, TB, Malaria, and Saharan famine.

But wait, no … I did not know most African airlines were forbidden from entering European airspace – fancy that! Neither did I realise how much uranium went missing from Niger's mines. No, I had no idea that Chad's air force bombed the Taureg rebels back to the mountains every year, but sure, I had heard of westerners getting kidnapped in Africa. I read newspapers.

Well, yes, when she put it like that, I guess I could understand why no insurance company would want to insure me – for any amount of money. Quite so!

In short, I was uninsurable. Most countries where Celtel International were planning to send me, were on blacklists for war, corruption, bad roads, catastrophic airlines – you name it, they had it!

Boarding the plane to Accra, Ghana, en route to Freetown, Sierra Leone, who knew I would still be living in Africa 15 years later? I had no inkling that an emergency evacuation was what it would take to get me out of the country and back on European soil. I was also blissfully unaware that it would take six months of chasing DHL packages, signing documents, and passport copies before my company was sorted and I could get my first payment.

Au contraire! Enjoying Celtel's travel policy, I sat in the Business Class lounge and sipped my wine, smiling. I could get used this, I thought, ignoring the butterflies.

NOT SO MUCH LIKE THE TRAVEL BROCHURES

Freetown, Sierra Leone, is one of West Africa's largest deepwater ports. Founded in 1792 as a colony for freed slaves who fought for the Brits in the American Revolutionary War, it is located at the western end of the Gulf of Guinea. Tropical storms forming over the Congo basin dump tons of water on Sierra Leone before heading out to the Atlantic Ocean en route to the Caribbean. In Sierra Leone, the soil is red, rich and fertile. The ground is full of diamonds and the ocean full of fish.

At the centre of Freetown, in the middle of a roundabout, stands an enormous 500-year-old Cotton Tree, home to thousands of fruit bats. Five minutes away is a 20-km long beach. The beach road cuts between beach bars and the golf course. Back in 2000, the beach road was the way home from Paddy's (a restaurant and bar where most of Freetown's expats hanged out) to our company guesthouses.

There were three military checkpoints along the road manned by UN, ECOWAS (Economic Community of West African states), and British troops. When I arrived in January 2000, the curfew was 9 pm – 6 pm. All land outside Freetown was rebel territory and a "no go" zone.

My driver, Barry, had an old brown Toyota with welded brackets on the windscreen to prevent theft and two bullet holes on the passenger side. Barry, a businessman before the civil war started, had lost everything but knew everyone. Driving me around was his way of getting capital to start over again, a resilience I saw all over Freetown. Never give up. What a life lesson!

Freetown was in limbo. Food was scarce. Commodities were limited. Electricity was sporadic.

Our managing director, Howard Martindale, rented a mansion that doubled up as company guesthouse. A passage around a central courtyard had access to five guest rooms. We kept chickens and goats and grew vegetables. Now and again, the local shop got a delivery of bacon. We worked and lived together. A typical day ended with a sunset ocean swim, some beers at Paddy's and a communal dinner at home.

Mats, the project director helping me get started, left after a week. Now it was up to me but I had not the foggiest idea what to do.

I said as much to Thomas when I finally managed to get through on the phone.

"Didn't Mats help you with the project plan?"

"Yes, but that was just a plan. How do I ensure I build the cell sites correctly? How do I get everything to work? How can I be sure I select the best location? How do I get the switch site and main office connected with the shop and the city office, just for starters?"

"For fuck's sake," said Thomas.

"So, when are you coming to Freetown?" I asked. When Thomas employed me, he had promised to come and help me every month or so.

"Who knows? I have a lot to do in Gabon and Congo. Just build the fucking network!" he said.

Right! With those inspiring words, I sat down and devised a strategy. I treated all elements as black boxes. What they contained was not important. I focused on where they physically belonged and how they connected to the rest of the equipment. I started drawing and identifying what each box needed for input and what it delivered as output. I asked questions of all the local staff and contractors.

Ericsson's power people taught me more about generators and equipment shelters than I ever wanted to know. From Celtel's network planners I picked up the basics of cell planning and transmission planning. The local staff and I found out all we needed for building permits and aviation clearance. Over the phone and via faxes, Thomas taught me number planning and how to interconnect with an international gateway. IT contractors helped me define and plan the data network between offices.

The learning curve was steep. There was no mobile network. Phones and e-mails worked sporadically. All discussions were conducted face to face. I drove to all the sites twice a day to check the progress. Small decisions that should have taken a one-minute phone call took two hours. The work was very hands on. Of course, I knew every site inside out. When Ericsson's installers arrived, I knew exactly where I wanted the kit.

"Between this bullet hole and that bullet hole," was a typical instruction.

After three months, a basic but functional network covered half of Freetown. The billing system had not arrived yet and we ran the network on test SIM cards. Overnight we became the hottest ticket in town. All embassies, government departments, NGOs and the military commanders wanted mobile communications.

Our MD, Howard Martindale, struck a great deal with them; you can get a SIM card but no billing records. Whatever we bill, you pay! Once the proper SIMs are in country, you will need to come and swap. This simple business model had some unexpected outcomes, such as the British Commander's fury when the network had to be switched off for a few hours. We had only 200 test SIMs in circulation and thousands new proper SIM cards in the shop, awaiting buyers. But we couldn't sell them until the billing system went live and for that we needed to switch off the network. The Commander refused.

Howard told me to deal with it as he didn't get anywhere.

I braced myself for the call. This would be tricky. The British forces and the High Commission paid well. I needed to switch off the system for a few hours and get the billing system online. One of us had to fold.

In came the call.

"Yes Sir?" That was my only contribution to the 10-minute monologue.

Finally I managed to get a word in. "Sir, let me see if I have this correct. You have on-going military operations, right?"

"Yes."

"You are using Celtel's network for your communications?"

"Yes."

"Your soldiers are out chasing rebel units?"

"Yes, that's exactly why you cannot switch off the network."

"I can't switch the network off because you need to communicate with your units in the field?"

"Yes," he barked.

"So, you're telling me your troops are lying in ambush, waiting for the phone to ring?"

I knew I had him. I knew he would realise how ridiculous his request sounded.

Silence. His Sandhurst education prevented a barrage of choice superlatives.

"Not really," came the terse reply. He knew he had lost this round. "So, you can guarantee the network will be back up by 2 pm?"

"Yes, Sir."

FREETOWN HEATS UP

From our penthouse balcony in central Freetown, we could look down at the mayhem in the streets below. We had returned from Paddy's an hour earlier, just before the curfew.

The weather was hot and humid, the mood tense. Rumours were rife. From Howard's security briefing at the British High Commission, we knew some of the facts. Rebel forces had surrounded and disarmed a unit of UN Forces. They had taken their uniforms and vehicles, without a shot fired!

The UN troops had gone to war in sunglasses and air-conditioned Land Cruisers. When they got out of their cars, their shades fogged up and they couldn't see a thing. Dressed and equipped like UN troops, the rebels were now bearing down on Freetown.

People – most remembered the unspeakable atrocities carried out last time the rebels took over Freetown – were all at Lungi or Hasting's airports, trying to get out.

My phone rang. "Yes?"

It was Howard. "Get the fuck out of there and over to the guesthouse. The place is going south. Pack your bags. We need to evacuate," he said.

I looked at my watch. 10 pm. There was gunfire in the background.

"Sorry, Howard, we can't move now. The curfew is on and I can't risk running the checkpoints with all these trigger-happy ECOWAS troops around."

"Then, get here first thing tomorrow," he barked. "I want everyone in one location. Call me if there's a problem."

The next four days we spent holed up in the guesthouse. The mornings started with Barry and myself going around to the cell sites, siphoning diesel out of drums to keep the generators running and the network going. The rest of the days we spent burping diesel, playing cards and listening to sporadic bursts of gunfire until it was time for the evening refuel run.

The rebel faction leader, Foday Sankoh, lived up the road from our guesthouse and AK47s, RPG rockets and pistols – all fired without much aim – constantly whistled overhead.

Six nationalities holed up in confined quarters under tense conditions make for interesting group dynamics. Boredom, anxiety, concerns from families thousands of miles away, an inability to control your own security, unconfirmed rumours, and an abundance of whiskey can all add up to a toxic environment. It was time to get people out of the house.

I made a point of ensuring that everyone got information directly. I invited people out with me on the refuel runs. I even organized a round of evacuation golf (the course was next to the predefined evacuation points).

THE GREAT EVACUATIONS

I looked around our designated evacuation point, an empty field lined with palms. Something felt wrong. The British High Commission had called a general evacuation but we were only 20 or so standing around. British Paratroopers had secured the airport and some parts of Freetown. Cars swerved around corpses lining the road from the previous night's heavy fighting. I heard the whop-whop of double rotors as a Chinook helicopter dropped a team of paratroopers in the far end of the field and left again.

A lieutenant in camouflages loaded down by a huge pack and gun walked up to me.

"Are you in charge here?"

I looked around. "I guess so."

"OK, well, this area is secured now."

This was not good news. "We have been here over an hour," I said. "Isn't this where the British are evacuating from?"

The lieutenant stared at me. "Are you insane? The British are evacuating from the Mamioko Hotel. There is a kilometre long queue outside already. You'd better get all your people out of here!"

He turned around and walked back to his men.

Later that night, on the evening news in Sweden, my sister watched me walking up the ramp of the last Chinook leaving Freetown.

We eventually discovered we were heading for Dakar, Senegal. I called Ericsson's project manager, Mats, back in Sweden at around 3 am and confirmed the list of Ericsson's staff with me. He booked flights from Dakar for us all.

In Dakar, the airline offices swarmed with thousands of people trying to find flights. Everything was chaos. Over the phone, Mats gave me a list of names, airlines and booking references. Ericsson had not been able to pay the flights from Sweden and none of their contractors had enough money to pay their own tickets. Thank God for credit cards, as we had given Howard, who stayed behind, all the cash dollars we had on us. As we went from airline to airline, I yelled out names and references over the crowd. When a clerk found the booking, I sent my credit card over and got tickets back. We flew out that afternoon.

Mats called and asked me if I thought the Ericsson staff needed to see a psychologist when they landed. I said they were ok and if anything, they probably needed a detox from all whisky they drunk. That was my biggest mistake of the evacuation. Later I discovered from some Swedish news articles and feedback from Ericsson, that some people had been shaken to the core by the experience. One of the guys couldn't go back to work for several years. Seeing a psychologist as they came off the plane could have solved future personal issues. My great idea of taking people out and around Freetown hadn't worked for everyone. We all cope with pressure differently but never underestimate the impact of post-traumatic stress. The symptoms can pop up years afterwards. We live and learn ...

Eight weeks later, when the British troops had dispatched the rebels, I headed back to Sierra Leone from my project planning work in Chad.

Instead of using the normal Celtel two-day procedure to fly via Europe to a neighbouring African country, I decided to go across the continent. Big mistake!

I discovered on arrival in Abidjan, Ivory Coast, that the flight to Freetown no longer existed. Outside the arrival hall, thousands of people were trying to get into the airport. Abidjan's streets were deserted but I managed to flag down a lone taxi and went to the

Sofitel Hotel. Later I met a fellow refugee. Between us, we practically polished off the hotel bar's entire contents!

Phones did not work. Credit card machines were offline and there was no Internet. No one knew where I was. After five days, my fellow refugee and I started to get a bit tired of it all. Eventually, with the help of some dollars, I got a flight to Monrovia in Liberia. From Freetown's airport a short helicopter flip across the harbour saw me back at the guesthouse where we had left Howard.

How you may react during an evacuation all depends on the circumstances. In Indonesia, my girlfriend, being Chinese, was part of the target of rioters wanting a share of their business wealth. A mob wanting to steal, rape, and plunder, surrounded her complex.

I was powerless to help and seethed with frustration. In Sierra Leone, the situation felt more controlled even though more arms were involved. Not being as emotionally involved with the staff I had to take care of, I functioned more rationally.

The same way American dollars had secured the chartered evacuation flight from Jakarta for all Ericsson staff back in 98, cash saved me when I was alone and stuck in the Ivory Coast.

Ironically, being alone with no one else to think about made me calmer.

OUT ON A LIMB

I was enjoying a vacation at Raffles Hotel in Singapore when Thomas Jonell called to ask if I could take over the Tanzanian project. He said they wanted me to replace their "useless" project manager and then launch within a month.

The Tanzania project was Celtel's crown jewel, the largest network build we ever attempted. Country wise, it was a prime posting with tropical beaches, an established marina, diving, the Serengeti, Ngorongoro Crater and safaris galore. The large established expatriate community enjoyed the stable democracy and booming economy.

"Fine," I told Thomas. "Just ensure the current Project Director has left before I arrive." I wanted to start fresh on a clean slate. And so the stage was set.

In Dar es Salaam, my eyes roamed over the assembled project team. What a mess! The project had been going for five months but the team leaders had achieved nothing. As for launching the Dar es Salaam project within a month, there were two chances of that happening – fat and slim.

"So, you think all is on track then, do you?"

Ignoring the nods and murmurs of agreement, I continued: "We do not have a single lease signed for the cell sites. The radio network planner is doing marketing surveys. The transmission planner is doing the radio plan. We cannot build a single site as a result. The South African civil works contractor and his staff have been sitting here for weeks. What the flying fuck have you guys been doing for five months?"

Silence. I shook my head.

"Go home, guys," I said.

I needed to pull the handbrake on the project, re-plan, review, and start all over again.

I walked into the former Project Director's office. He and his secretary had isolated themselves in the last room down the corridor and put reflective film on the glass panes. Understandable, since they had been having an affair, but there was zero connection with the rest of the team.

I sat down and started looking through some files. There was no sign of any paperwork, no budget or network plans. I called Thomas. People had flown in every second week from both the Amsterdam head office and the support office in South Africa. What the hell had they been doing?

A furious Thomas booked a flight from Amsterdam to Tanzania straight away.

I found two more ticking bombs. Firstly there was no budget approval by Celtel for towers, generators, shelters, civil works, contractors, project staff salaries, expenses, office refurbishment, the switch room construction, IT equipment or travel. Nothing! Secondly, the current cash burn was around USD 100 000 per week for hotel rooms, daily allowances, and phone bills. TTCL, the state-owned telephone operator and our partner in Tanzania shared our premises with an internet connection point less than 10 meters away but no one had signed off the cost of getting a server and pulling some cables. Instead they used their South African and UK phones to surf the Internet while roaming and Celtel picked up the bills. Unbelievable!

The next two weeks were madness. I had to restructure the project – stop everything, regroup and start over! The first thing I did was rearrange where people sat. My management style is open, accessible and direct. I like to lead by example. However, democracy has no place in a project with defined scope, tasks and timelines.

Each functional team got a room sequenced by task flow. General teams got a desk in the open planned big office area. I placed myself so I could see everything going on and everyone could see me.

On the functional side, I divided up the project team into logical units – admin, site acquisition, civil works, radio and transmission planning, core network planning, finance, imports, logistics, project management – and applied my 'black box approach' to each unit.

We documented all input, output and processes, creating files to collect all contracts, approvals, drawings and equipment lists.

I tied the purse strings tighter, sending contractors home since there was nothing yet to build. To rent a house or apartment, each long-term consultant was given half of what a hotel room currently cost us. They were welcome to share.

I identified each item needed, estimated costs, and renegotiated contracts. Instead of Celtel being an open-ended check, each contractor now had a budget per site. This was all added onto a spreadsheet so we could track three values – estimated, contracted and actual. At any given time, I knew exactly where we were with the budget.

Thomas and I took away all the micro details. We broke the network down in logical blocks and areas based on their geographical location and how we could link them via the transmission network. HQ and Switch Room got their own sections.

Everything fitted onto one A3 sheet. Instead of each unit doing their own survey of an area, we created 'road shows', representing all functions that affected a site selection. All aspects were documented and photographed. I reported progress weekly based on when we could commercially launch an area instead of technical micro details.

The team gelled into a well-oiled machine. There was now a purpose and tangible goal. I fired the old project planner and civil works managers, making all the other unit heads accountable for their tasks. Philippe Ambonguilat, our HQ architect from Gabon, rose to the challenge of building the HQ he had designed. Marjo Baayen, the new planner, became my second-in-command.

Armed with new plans, new budget and a boosted morale, we set to work. Within three months, we had launched Dar es Salaam with 20 sites (October 2001). Six months later, we had built another 100 sites across Tanzania, all ahead of time and below budget.

TOO MANY CHIEF'S

Everyone wanted to be associated with Celtel Tanzania's high profile network build. After the initial restructuring and re-planning, people from HQ in Holland and our support office in South Africa flew in and out with different ideas of what my team should do and how they should do it. All with good intent, but sadly this created confusion among the team.

Who was the boss? My managers from HQ and I had different opinions. To ensure consistent directions and focus, I again had to put a protective bubble around the project team.

My team did what I wanted them to do. If something went wrong, it was my fault, but that's part of being the boss. If you give someone the responsibility of a task, ensure you give him the authority to perform it. Not everyone accepted this.

During one heated discussion, I said to the latest seagull manager pecking at my jurisdiction:

"If you want to run the project, have it! I'll be on tonight's flight to Europe!"

I walked back to my desk, shrugged and started packing. Enough with pulling 18 to 20-hour days against a constant stream of seagull managers swooping in and trying to change everything we had achieved! I'd reached the end of my tether!

However, I gave myself some time to cool off and after a while, Mr Seagull and I sat down and resolved how we could better work together.

During its 10-month set-up, Celtel Tanzania went through three managing directors – each with their own inconsistent reporting requirements, each with their own views on how we should build the network.

Instead of reporting progress on details on each site, I indicated when different cities and areas were up and running so that the marketing and sales department could plan their commercial launches and activities.

Financial reporting requirements changed as our Finance Director built up his department and got systems and procedures in place. After initial arguments about permissions to sign off payments from the project budget, which was much larger than the company's start-up budget, we settled into a nice routine, even though he had no say in how I spent the money. Once city after city launched and revenue started flowing into the coffers, he relaxed.

I signed the contracts. Finance Department captured them in their system. I approved supplier payments based on progress. They effected the payments. I built sites. They logged them into the asset register. I spent money. They tried to keep costs down – a good working relationship.

Control over money is a strong powerbase within a company. The project operated outside the company's structures but affected its internal control procedures – not a great situation for most finance directors to deal with, I do agree.

Celtel Tanzania's hierarchical HR policies were causing friction in my team. I had to implement policies that aligned to how we worked. The friction was now between the HR team and me while my guys could get on with the job.

For example, the travel policy linked hotel room standards and food allowances to job grading. I don't think it's fair to send a team into the field when they cannot all stay in the same hotels or afford to eat at the same restaurants.

I implemented a bonus scheme based on the team's performance and targets, not individuals. I paid the bonuses when we reached our targets and not end of the year.

I took the cap off cell phone spending and empowered my team members to take decisions. Nobody played the blame game. If something went wrong, we solved it as a team.

Most of my changes went against Celtel Tanzania's company policies and Tanzanian culture, creating a flat and equal organisation within a hierarchical culture. It worked!

Corporate politics often reared its head. Peers blamed others instead of doing their own jobs. The minutes from our weekly joint status meetings often saved my bacon.

At our launch of the Dar es Salaam network, several managers from HQ flew in to celebrate with the company directors and local shareholders. That afternoon, our MD requested my attendance at the dinner. I declined, having already planned a party to thank my team.

The MD insisted I attend the dinner. I refused, determined to spend the evening with my team. The argument teetered back and forth until Sir Allan Rudge, Celtel International's CEO, walked up and said: "I understand your decision. I would have done the same." Parting, he added, "Well done! Please thank the team from me."

It was a small gesture that meant a lot to my team and me.

It was a sad day when we closed the project and dissolved the best team I've ever had the privilege to lead.

KNOW WHAT YOU'RE BUILDING!

Was he serious? Thomas had flown in to Ouagadougou to check on progress with the network and HQ build in Burkina Faso. Walking around the skeleton of a building that was Celtel Burkina Faso's HQ, he pointed out flaws without pause.

"Per, what have you been doing?"

"Building according to the plans you gave me," I answered.

"I never approved this, for example," he said, pointing at a window in an odd, angled wall cutting across a corner.

I pulled out three sheets of faxed papers from my folder.

"Isn't that your signature in the bottom right hand corner?"

I handed him the drawings.

"*Jo. Men för faan, så här ska det ju inte se ut,*" he exclaimed in Swedish. (Loosely translated as: For fuck's sake, that's exactly how it shouldn't look!) We sat down and went through everything in detail, reworking certain aspects.

Nigel Jacobs, a CCTV and access control contractor from the UK wandered over as we were working on the drawings and dropped another bombshell.

"Guys, you might have a problem here," he said. "The construction workers think they are building a hotel."

"You're fucking joking!"

He wasn't. We found more oddities – no signed agreement between the building owner and Celtel, even after the MD had guaranteed it was all in place. It wasn't. Eventually, HQ in Holland fired the MD.

When designing and constructing the sites for the core network equipment, we installed two power circuits. A normal one for when commercial power was available and one critical for running the core on generators. The critical circuit powered the switch and other core elements as well as all the air-conditioning needed to keep the equipment cool in the sweltering African heat. The normal circuit powered all non-essential stuff, like lights, office air conditioners, etc. This was standard practice.

The MD in Chad demanded that his office air-conditioner be on the critical link. I refused. He insisted. HQ in Holland fired this MD as well.

In Tanzania, the local electrician overseeing the power installation for the switch, followed Tanzanian regulations and installed a breaker switch between the battery back-up units and the equipment. It took us a day to identify the problem and find the breaker when the entire network lost all power. Someone had done the normal thing and switched off all breakers when leaving the building. No one got fired that time.

GRACE UNDER PRESSURE IN UGANDA

"There you are, you bugger!" Howard Martindale's clipped British vowels assailed me as I walked into the Ugandan project office. "You wanted it. It is yours. I'm leaving."

Seriously? I had been looking forward to upgrading the Celtel Uganda network with Howard, my former MD in Sierra Leone, but he leaves as I arrive. WTF?

Thomas later explained that head office had decided to pull Howard out to avoid having two directors on one project.

Uganda was a disappointment, especially after the emotional high of the Tanzania project. The network was in shocking condition.

Subscribers left in droves but nobody knew why and nobody seemed to care.

One morning – at 3 am, to be precise – my phone rang.

Praveena Raman, our radio network planner in charge of integrating new sites had bad news. They were supposed to integrate five new sites into the Kampala network, but despite their best efforts, they could not get the new sites to work with the old network.

"Nothing bloody works," she said.

"How long before you need to start the roll-back?" I asked. Back then, when you added new sites, the network was off line. New configuration files were loaded and the network restarted. We needed to be live again by 5 am latest.

"In about an hour, but I doubt it will work. Something is wrong."

Shit, we had two hours left.

"Skip the new sites. Start the roll-back now," I said. I hung up. Tried to go back to sleep.

We spent the next three days digging until we found the problem. Siemens had done a network swap-out about six months previously and replaced all old equipment with new kit. Instead of the configuration files designed for Kampala, they had loaded a standard set. Neighbouring sites did not link with each other, which made dropped calls the norm, rather than the exception. While Praveena and her team reset all the parameters for the correct radio network plan, I called Siemens in South Africa and lambasted them. I felt a little better after that.

FIRST MAN IN!

Niamey, capital of Niger: midday and the atmosphere was like a furnace at just under 50 degrees Celsius. As usual, there was no power, so no air con. Sweat ran down my arms onto the towel around my laptop, while I was having a conversation with the boss on speakerphone so that the Celtel's Finance Director, Nick Kamperdijk, could also hear the conversation.

"Per, you are not the MD," said Omari Issa, Chief Operating Officer for Celtel. With more than 20 years' experience at IFC and the World Bank – Celtel's largest funder – Omari was part of Celtel's shift towards operating the networks we had built all over Africa, instead of us just chasing new licenses and building new networks. All Celtel's MDs in Africa reported to Omari. While I was in Niger setting up the company, another team was busy with setting up Tanzania. These two countries would be the last green field networks Celtel built.

Nick shook his head and lit another cigarette.

"I never claimed to be MD," I replied, rolling my eyes at Nick. "But I need these papers and signatures to register the company for taxes, PAYE and insurances."

"That is the MD's job and you are not the MD. Your job is to build a network," Omari retorted.

"I know, but as the Project Director and the first man in here, my role is to set everything up until the MD arrives or until you appoint one. When do you think that might be?"

"We have not appointed the MD yet."

This discussion was going nowhere. We hung up.

Nick laughed. "You'll never win this one," he said.

I sighed. Every discussion with Omari went nowhere. Progress had come to a standstill. There was no approved budget for the initial build and no signed contracts, so who knew when the equipment would arrive? No MD had been appointed so there was no one to hand over to. I hung in limbo and Omari and I never did manage to have a constructive discussion about it.

Niger, in the southern part of Sahara, offers desert sand dunes in the north and savannah in the south. Niamey, the capital, situated along the Niger River, had few tarred roads. Camels mingled with people on the streets and in the markets. The desertification of the landscape provided a pale contrast to the colourful dresses and headscarves worn by the Huasa and Taureg women, tall people who carried themselves with pride.

I arrived with a bag of cash and a piece of paper with the name and phone number of our local partner scrawled on it. I knew nothing of Niger but had to build a mobile network for the company. This was the real African frontier, all right.

Within Celtel, the unwritten rule was that the first person of the start-up team coming into a country took the role of MD just to set up finances, company structures and get project, marketing and operations going. Once the appointed MD arrived, he would take over.

The first hurdles were accommodation, office space, bank account, communications and money. The first three turned out to be easy. I arranged two rooms in a hotel by the river. One was for me to sleep in, the other served as our office, and I sorted out a bank account within a few days.

Communications were a nightmare. The local telecom operator's Internet service did not function. To get hold of Thomas Jonell, my boss, I had to call our office in London and ask the secretary to call him in Holland and have him call me. Status reports, check requisitions, contracts and any other question or request, all went the same circuitous route via fax. At least it created a paper trail no one could fiddle with.

Nick had arrived after two months. In just three days he had gone through my finance binders, got accounting software in and was helping me with the remaining corporate tasks. Khalil, the Project Director I had trained in Burkina Faso, took over the building of the network and the office refurbishment. The marketing department was in training and we had agreed with the city government for billboard locations. I camped out in the reception of the telecom's minister to get our number plan signed off.

When an appointed MD finally arrived, he was less than impressed with me. I realised that by failing to sit down with Omari and clarify my role and his expectations, I had ended up in his bad books. Lesson learnt. I decided I was due for a vacation.

THE DARKER SIDE OF AFRICA

Africa is a continent of extremes. Africans have strong opinions they are not afraid to vocalise and a disagreement can easily escalate out of control. Some of my contractors loved Africa. Others hated it. Some felt homesick. Others behaved like spoilt little despots.

I recall feeling so disgusted by the greed of certain directors who spent two hours arguing over their wives' phone allowance – a few hundred dollars – at a weekly ExCo meeting in front of local

Tanzanian employees who had no phone allowance at all, that I walked out.

I was especially cross when I thought about how all the directors drove 4x4 Toyota Land Cruisers, lived in mansions and had their kids in private schools – all paid for by the company.

Even though bribery, corruption, and racism exist all over the world, they are very obvious in Africa.

Bribery and Corruption:

In Africa, a whopping US$ 148 billion (around 25% of Africa's GDP) disappeared through bribery and corruption, according to the World Bank report from early 2013.

Are your friends, colleagues and managers as ethical as you think? And where do you draw the line? What are you prepared to do for business?

What do you do when someone offers you 100 000 US dollars just for your signature? Think about what that cash could buy you – school and university fees sorted, a new car or holiday … do you take it? Would your answer be different if it was one million US dollars?

When is something a bribe and when is it just considered a gift? In Nigeria, a flat screen TV is a gift. In Sweden it would be a bribe. In some countries the corruption is so rife and open, that even the security guards requires a payment to let you into buildings so you can attend your meeting.

How do you keep your morals when they could hamper your company's business prospects? How can you report one staff member, when the whole organisation is in on it? How can you remain anonymous when you need to give so much evidence that only a blind guy wouldn't figure out who reported you? In the end, it boils down to your own integrity.

Just remember that once you start taking bribes, you are stuck in a vicious cycle. I ended up blacklisting the companies that offered me bribes. I prefer to sleep peacefully rather than having to watch my back.

Social Values and Racism:

When we venture outside our comfort zones, our social norms can change. How do we teach our children values? Simply by maintaining our own, which brings me to racism. Having been brought up in Sweden with its strict adherence to racial and sexual equality, working in Africa took me by surprise.

My boss came into the office, furious with his young son who had thrown an empty milk carton on the floor while having breakfast. When told to pick it up, the kid replied, "The maid will do that."

Where will these attitudes lead when he grows up?

In Sierra Leone, rebels had burnt down the State House, smashed up the local telephone company and local brewery, and chopped off hands all over the place, yet I felt perfectly safe. The Freetown locals knew where I lived, where I worked and socialised.

By treating everyone with equal respect, I was able to walk through areas my local subcontractors would visit only with bodyguards. I experienced the same friendliness from the locals in Chad, Burkina Faso and Niger.

While building a network in Tanzania, I experienced internal racism between local Tanzanians and Indian immigrants. It was subtle, but many carried a mutual distrust and hatred towards the other. As an expat you will likely experience some form of racism. Don't buy into it.

Mo Ibrahim, a Sudanese (of the Ibrahim Index) and Moez Daya, a Kenyan, built Celtel into a pan African mobile operator based on equal values and integrity, but having to listen to some of the contractors slating the local workers purely on race, disgusted me. Some so much that I sent them home.

IN SHORT

- When the chips are down, cash is always king! Ensure you have enough on you.

- Democracy does not work in a project, but stand up for your staff. Only in victory are your transgressions forgiven.

- Don't be afraid to ask for help and get all instructions in writing. Verbal agreements are easy and comfortable, but people conveniently forget.

- Ensure that whatever your project builds works for the people who have to run it after you leave.

- Keep abreast of all changes in head office. Ensure you and your manager have the same goals. At the very least, ensure you understand his!

- If you go through a traumatic event, like an evacuation, car crash, bomb blast, etc., take time and see a physiologist afterwards. Ensure that any of your staff having similar experiences do the same.

KNOW WHEN TO LEAVE

Of all the stratagems, to know when to quit is the best. – Chinese
Proverb

When working in Africa, I pulled long hours. While friends and colleagues socialised, I sat in the office until midnight. Once the work slowed down, my bosses would move me to another country and project. While I enjoyed the work, I realised it was not fitting into my life plans.

I have seen many foreigners sitting in their bars, lodges, farmhouses in southern France, or driving an overland truck across continents wearing that look of "Hmmm, it didn't turn out the way I planned".

Places change. We change. Travel is all about timing.

"Get your skinny arse over here!" George Aylmer's broad American twang made me smile.

"Hi George, nice to hear from you too," I said. "How's Egypt?"

"It's full of fucking sand! Per, I need your help here. The logistics is in a mess not even you could create!"

"I'm in Indonesia for another couple of months," I replied.

"Yeah, but Indonesia's finances have gone tits up. Make a plan."

George was right. The currency had lost 80-90% of its value. No one could afford telecoms equipment. We all had started looking for new jobs in other markets. Some had already left. I was in limbo. George's call was welcome.

Some phone calls to head office and a few weeks later, I was in a taxi heading for Cairo. Coming from lush and tropical Jakarta, Egypt felt dry, dusty, bleak, and sandy. Only the minarets calling Muslims to prayers felt familiar – Indonesia having the world's largest Muslim population. Seven months later, I would decline a 20% salary increase and an amazing bonus scheme.

Egypt for me was hard. I'm an early bird, in the office around 7 am. I like to knock off when the day's tasks are done, meet friends for a beer or dinner and then be in bed well before midnight. This does not work in the Egyptian culture where you sleep after work before meeting friends for a drink at 10 pm, and eating dinner around midnight. By the time my Egyptian friends were meeting up, I was already in bed. The project was hectic. We worked around the clock seven days a week to get the network up in time, but I enjoyed it. I worked in Egypt and lived my dream!

One evening George and I sat on my 23rd floor balcony in Zamalek, Cairo, overlooking the Nile. Feet propped up on the railing we watched the sun disappear behind the pyramids of Giza – a million dollar view. I had chased my dream so hard and achieved my goal, but was working around the world really worth the sacrifices? Two thoughts vied for my attention: 'What now?' and 'Where to from here?' I felt lost and couldn't ignore the sinking feeling in my stomach.

I sipped a pensive whiskey. The ice clinked in the glass over the evening sounds of people, donkeys and cars.

"What's up?" asked George.

"I don't want to be doing this anymore,"

I could see confusion in George's face. "I forgive you for dragging me to this sandy car-infested city from Indonesia," I said only half joking, "but I've achieved my goal. I've worked around the world. And now I really, really, need to do something new."

George tried to point out I hadn't been to America, nor had I seen the rest of Africa. It didn't help. The sinking feeling was still there.

This would not be the last time I would decide to "quit while ahead" as the old saying goes.

"Per, do you have a minute?" asked Jonas Gramer, the new boss of the Project Managers at Ericsson in Sweden.

"Sure. What's up?"

"Remember how we discussed you taking six months leave of absence to go and work for an operator?"

"Yes?"

I had just signed with Celtel International, Dutch company, to build the mobile network in Sierra Leone one week earlier. I had flown home from Philippines to sign the papers and my flight to Freetown left in a couple of days. Was something wrong?

"Well, HR have changed their policies and no longer approve the move," said Jonas, looking into his coffee cup.

"What? Well, in that case, I resign," I blurted out.

"You don't need to be so drastic," Jonas said.

"You give me no choice," I retorted. "I signed an agreement. I have my tickets to Freetown and I leave in a couple of days."

"But you have to give three months' notice."

"Fine. I resign and I'll take the leave owing to me."

A quick check with HR confirmed I had accrued more than 80 days leave.

We looked at each other. Jonas shrugged.

"Good Luck, Per!"

Ten minutes later, my resignation signed, I walked out of the doors – five years to the day, I had first walked in through the same doors.

Of course, later over a coffee, I wondered whether I had done the right thing, walking away from five years with Ericsson on a snap decision. But the GSM rollout heydays in Asia were over. The initial spirit of 'Just Do It' was out. Cost cuttings and consensus management was in.

I had learnt a lot from Ericsson and I had given it my all, but it was time to move on and do something new!

Again, in Uganda, after three hectic and intense years with Celtel, I had the urge to leave.

Managing a network is like directing an orchestra. It involves constant checks, tweaks and adjustments. Check log files, error reports, statistics. Tweak. Adjust. Do quality tests. Ensure the network is designed around users movement and changing behaviour. Before we arrived to do some expansions, the Ugandan network had slipped into disarray.

In order to do our job, we needed the network to work properly and had to add more work to the projects scope to fix it. Once done, we had transformed it from the worst network in Kampala to the best. The damage to the Celtel image would take a lot longer to repair.

At the same time, I was in discussions with HQ about upcoming projects in Angola and Mozambique. Repairing a network with old second hand equipment was not my ideal. I wanted something new and sexy.

There was lots of fun stuff to do in Kampala – clay pigeon shooting, rafting the Bujagali falls at the start of the Nile, exploring national parks, dining at old colonial hotels, visiting Jane Goodall's chimpanzee sanctuary on Ngamba Island, watching flies swarms over Victoria Lake like sheets of rain. So why did I feel so depressed?

Alone at the Blue Mango restaurant, I ordered another beer and took stock.

Yes, I was earning good money, enjoying a cool job, and a life of adventure, but I had nobody to share it with. Three years of living in hotel rooms had reduced my life to a suitcase, laptop bag, and some golf clubs. I felt exhausted after working 16 to 20-hour days.

Worse, the telecoms environment had gone from a friendly environment where suppliers, clients, colleagues and competitors helped each other, to a situation where people now stabbed one another in the back. Did I still fit in at Celtel International? What other options did I have?

Well, I could buy cheap yachts in South Africa, sail to Europe and sell them. I could work for a supplier installing biometric security systems in African airports. I could take a few years off and travel through South and Central America. I could start a Mobile Value Added Services Company in South Africa. I could carve out my own destiny ...

I ordered another beer, returned to the office and emailed my letter of resignation to Thomas.

IN SHORT

- Know what you want. Be honest with yourself. Money won't necessarily buy you a good life.
- Follow your heart and your gut! Quit while you're ahead.

RUNNING YOUR OWN MULTI-NATIONAL SHOW

"Screw it. Let's do it!" – Richard Branson, 1997

"What do you think?" asked my friend Wayne, a salesman who organised golf tournaments in Philippines and Thailand, as we hung out at the Manila Southwoods Golf and Country Club.

We had just met with the founders of Xurpas Inc – three young Filipino guys with great ideas, and fantastic technology.

"Dunno, let's do the numbers again," I said.

We applied Xurpas' figures, penetration rates, and user behaviour statistics to what we knew of the three South African operators' data, halved the end user prices, decreased the estimated uptake and halved the result twice again.

"If we double the costs, we could still make good money but do we really know what we are doing?"

I looked at Wayne.

"Probably not," he replied. "Let's play a round of golf and then fly to South Africa."

A South African, three Filipinos and a Swede starting a business in Africa. It sounds like the start of a joke. And indeed, mixing the three cultures and nationalities had its challenges. None of us knew anything about selling mobile services in Africa and we had a business model that proved to be totally wrong for Africa.

We cold called mobile operators, FMCG (Fast-Moving Consumer Goods) and marketing companies. We had no external financing. We had no idea that our business model and proposed services were ahead of the mobile operators' technical capabilities. Once again, we had to learn about each Africa country's legislation and adapt our business model to every new technology and each mobile operator we provided services to.

We arrived in South Africa in September 2002 and so began the journey that took Starfish Mobile from an idea to an operation in 21 countries. We criss-crossed Africa, battling with costs and cash flow. We banged our heads against corporate bureaucracy and legislation. We almost went broke twice. We laughed, cried, and learnt!

GOING IT ALONE!

Africa is the last frontier. The risks and rewards are enormous but Africa – as anyone who has ever worked here will tell you – is not for wimps.

Founding Starfish Mobile without Venture Capital or external loans gave us freedom. It also gave us sleepless nights. Wayne and I had to ensure we had enough money to pay salaries, bills, investments and business expenses. We had to monitor our cash flow. We only paid ourselves a salary if we had enough funds.

Our cash flow was erratic due to payment cycles that varied from 30 days to eight months. Some clients could not pay monthly due to a lack of forex, others could pay only twice a year when their tobacco crops matured.

When we started Starfish Mobile in South Africa, we just thought it was a good idea with financial potential. We had no idea that it would become a pan-African company. Initially, the South African market had not been what we expected. The mobile operators' technology lacked features we needed and they were not as open to co-operation as we had expected.

We only had ourselves to blame for the lack of business-intelligence gathering from our side.

Needing more eggs in our revenue basket, we seized our first expansion opportunity in Congo DRC in mid-2003. After that, we added two to three new territories per year.

As Starfish Mobile expanded, we had to adapt. We had to change employees and skills in accordance with local legislations, currency rules, double taxation treaties, labour laws, equity rules for foreign nationals and varying accounting rules. Not all employees shared our vision. Many people just wanted a salary. And that's okay, too.

As we expanded into the continent, we realised that with more than 66 national cultures, groups, languages and cultures, it is impossible to treat Africa "as one". Not even East Africa, West Africa or southern Africa share common cultures.

As we built up the Starfish Mobile corporate culture from this multicultural mix, we learnt that each culture added a new dimension and put their mark on the company.

Today Starfish Mobile has subsidiaries in 10 countries. Each has different national and business cultures. When analysing a new opportunity, there are no set rules or processes, just a 'business check list' or 'cultural baseline' to analyse the pros and cons of all information we collected to build a business case. No two countries are alike. The list is constantly updated as we discover new things.

When we started expanding outside South Africa, people asked us why. "Because no one else was there," was our stock response. We could become a big fish in many small ponds. We could get the first mover advantage. Sure, we burnt our fingers, but we persevered.

PRUNING THE DEAD WOOD

When we started migrating the organisation from start-up to operational efficiency, we looked at all revenue streams, analysing cost, effort and time spent versus revenue generated. We identified dead wood and unprofitable deals – it's hard when you have a great relationship with unprofitable clients, but you have to break eggs to make an omelette.

If it did not generate a profit, we cut it. Nothing was sacred. The result was amazing. The overall workload for staff decreased. We now had time to focus on and increase the profitable deals. By doing less, we made more.

Entrepreneurs need to know that what works in Europe or Asia might not work in Africa. The continent has a reputation for bribery, corruption and a general lack of progress. The rules of business are different. Accepted standard business practices in Nigeria could land you in a European court.

Starfish Mobile succeeded in Africa, without Wayne and me having to resort to bribery, which goes to show that anything is possible. Sure, we could have progressed faster with some 'facilitation' but that is not what we are about. In Africa, you have to establish your own code of ethics.

At Starfish Mobile, the buck stopped with Wayne and me. Having no big organisation to provide support and cash made things scary. It was often touch and go but taking risks paid off.

SWIMMING WITH SHARKS

Greed defines most corporate cultures as we have seen in a recent spate of suicidal bankers and high profile names getting done for ethical misconduct. Disgruntled employees spill the beans. Tax authorities question the books.

Sooner or later the truth about unethical behaviour will come out. Legislation changes with each new discovery. How can you ensure the rules you follow today will not put you behind bars in five years?

Many corporates exploit gaps in legislation for monetary gains. They follow rules in one country in the full knowledge that such practises are illegal or unethical in their home countries.

In Starfish Mobile's line of business, spamming, and hidden subscriptions are typical of such practices. Companies get hold of a database and subscribe everyone to a service costing 50 US cents a day without permission. To complain or unsubscribe, users have to call a number in Australia, India, or wherever. When users click on a mobile advert, their mobile account suddenly starts losing 50 US cents a day due to a hidden subscription.

For companies like Starfish Mobile that run an ethical, transparent business, such behaviour can seriously threaten our image and products.

In any business, sharks will exploit a gap and vanish. You have to hope that the sharks are not your local subsidiaries as the brand image fallout could be disastrous. One rogue operation can ruin your entire corporate reputation.

At the same time, you will need to ensure that your local operations compete with a fair set of rules. It is a chess game of compromises. You need to define the boundaries – the rules no local operation can break – that ensure ethical accounting principles, quality operation, excellent client services, compliance with local legislation and best practice for long-term gains.

Select the strictest regulatory environment you operate in and base your corporate rules on that.

Once these umbrella rules are set from HQ, look at each territory. Work through the local legislation and business practices and set local rules. These will vary from country to country so be careful not to hamstring your operations. You want local partners to capitalise on the local knowledge of doing business there.

There will be compromises but ensure you hang on to your corporate image and rules. Do not allow rules to slide without proper analysis of consequences. Reputation is everything and building up a good brand image can take years. Losing it can take a few seconds.

HANDING OVER THE BATON

Running an expanding company is a constant compromise. You have to balance growth with revenues, investments with shareholder returns, sacrifice one opportunity for another, support existing local operations while starting new ones and prioritise resources. Jumping on opportunities and getting a strategic foothold in markets can be thrilling but when your resources get stretched, the novelty wears off.

I hope that your company survives and you realise you are no longer a start-up but have matured into an operational organisation. Operational efficiency must replace the original gung-ho culture. The focus must shift from expansions to revenue growth and stability. Operations and finance becomes more important than the team searching for new opportunities.

If you stay in the start-up mood, your company could fail to fulfil its commitments, lose market share and burn out.

By doing less, you can make more. It can be hard to let go of territories and decrease the footprint you worked hard to achieve, but it might be time for a new era.

It happened to Celtel International and it happened to Starfish Mobile.

After years of setting the company afloat, my head was abuzz with ideas for new ventures. The truth is, and research has shown, that founders who remain in the business can prevent the organisation from evolving.

Conversely, entrepreneurs who hand over their creation to a new set of managers are highly regarded in Europe or America, but not so much in Africa. People here don't understand why someone might build up and leave a thriving company. A common comment is "Why? It's your company. You built it."

You have to then explain that even as the founder you might not be the best person to run it.

I believe every company needs to regularly review and evaluate its management to ensure that the best team runs the show. As the company evolves from start-up to maturity, management must adjust to the changes. Shareholders of a company must ensure the best possible management team is in place at every phase.

Even so, there's no easy way to tell your shareholders you've decided to leave the company you helped build up. At the end of the day, you just have to come straight out and say it.

IN SHORT

If you want to start your own company, you must consider the following:

- Multiply by 10 whatever you think it will cost to start and run your company. If you have a family to support, have a couple of years of running expenses in the bank, both for the company and the family, as your salary is not a given.
- You will be under immense pressure. Be prepared for 18-hour days, seven days a week. Make sure your family or significant other understands this. The glitzy magazine covers and CNN reports on success stories never show the grunt work it took these people to get there or the multitude of failed ventures!
- Do not hamstring your local partners but set the corporate rules and operate within them.

- You have only one brand image. Protect your reputation at all costs.

- Sentimental values and attachments are not profitable. Step away from time to time and see yourself and the company objectively. Be honest. Be ruthless!

- Understand and embrace the difference between Western and African values. See them as refreshing!

- Remember, Africa is not backwards, just different.

- Always get the best person for the job. Accept that it might not be you.

- Select the strictest regulatory environment you operate in and base your corporate rules on that.

- Make the rules up as you go. Remember opportunity lies where few want to venture.

AFTER THOUGHTS

THE EXPAT PACKAGE – FINANCES AND TAX ISSUES

As an expat, job grading, the country hardship factor and the overall consumer price index will all affect your salary, bonus package, and lifestyle in the new country. Each local company and country is different. You need to engage with the local HR department and check with colleagues who live there to find out the details. Once you have signed your contract and arrived, it is almost impossible to change any of it.

A friend thought he had landed a great deal when he went to work in an African country but reality struck when he and his family arrived. School fees were not included and the house allowance was based on South African prices, not the local dollar-based house rentals he was forced to pay.

The company even cut him short on a phone allowance – all because he had been too proud to ask for advice. Within a year, he terminated his contract, telling me he ended up paying out more than he earned.

It might sound boring, but you have to read up on taxation rules. Where your salary is paid is important. In Taiwan, the company had to pay local income tax for contractors. That, combined with double taxation agreements, saved us a lot of money. Ericsson paid an additional amount on salaries and some expenses. At Celtel, we had to submit receipts before the company paid back our expenses but we also got a daily allowance.

Knowing how the structure affects your tax situation is crucial. You have to comply with local legislation wherever you find yourself. You need to understand your host country's excise duty and taxation rules. Too many people working abroad think everything will just solve itself. The taxman won't agree.

UNDERSTANDING LOCAL COSTS

When I moved to Manila in 1999, my apartment had a central air-conditioning system. The first month landed me a 3 500 US$ electricity bill - we switched it off. One colleague who went to live in a West African country with her two dogs got fired for spending US$ 25 000 on the dogs' move alone. Another bought jewellery on credit at a gold souk without realising the cost in relation to her salary. The company bailed her out and shipped her home.

I picked up a 1946 Harley Davidson for US$ 2 500 in Indonesia and bought myself a US$ 10 driver's license so I could ride it. In fact, I bought my first four driver's licenses.

A 4-star hotel in Congo DRC costing around US$ 400 per night would get you two or three hotel rooms in South Africa.

House rentals in Tanzania are linked to the US$ exchange rate. Tanzanian Shillings have lost 20% of their value against the US$ in the last few years, but contractors still earn in Tanzanian Shillings.

The list goes on. I also lost track of money and its worth. In Indonesia, I wanted to change a faulty remote control for the TV and came home with a new surround sound system instead.

Understanding local costs and the impact of exchange rate fluctuations is essential. The cost of living abroad can turn an adventure into a disaster.

ACCOMMODATION AND JOB GRADING

Your job grading will affect your house, car and furniture allowance. It affects which class you fly home on, which type of hotel room you stay in or whether you get a golf or gym membership. If your temporary home does not work for you, the entire contract can be a disaster. Ericsson paid for our stay in 5-star hotels. While working for Celtel in Africa, I stayed in company-rented guesthouses.

In Taiwan, I started out in a 5-star hotel but got bored after a month or two. My colleague Thomas Jonell, in Taiwan on a long-term contract, asked if I wanted to share an apartment with him. Close to restaurants and nightclubs, a five-minute walk to the office, dry cleaner and grocery store on the ground level, it was perfect for two workaholic bachelors!

Accommodation arrangements can vary but if you're going to be away from home a long time, it is only fair that the company you work for makes your away-time close to what you'd get at home.

UN, NGOs, AID AND COMPANIES

"By pouring money and goods into devastated regions, foreign aid workers sometimes compound the disruption and debauch the survivors."
– James Buchan

How does your organisation affect the local environment, culture and businesses? What happens when profit-driven companies compete with NGOs and Aid organisations? Can they co-exist? It's a touchy subject, especially in vast poverty stricken areas. We see suffering on the evening news. We donate money. We feel good. Few realise that by donating money they might have hampered a local company's potential.

Malawi, for example, had a few years of bad cotton production. The price soared and people could no longer afford clothes. The western world donated second-hand clothes in shiploads. By the time cotton production was restored, the local manufacturers could not compete with the donated loads of clothes. Today, many empty spinning factories are covered in cobwebs. Such good deeds killed a local industry.

In Sierra Leone, the UN troops thought they'd inject fresh money into the local economy by investing in local produce. They bought up so much fish from local fishermen that Sierra Leoneans could not find or afford to buy fish for themselves any more – their staple food with rice.

Big philanthropic icons donate mosquito nets to prevent the spread of Malaria without sparing a thought for the local mosquito net manufacturers they put out of business.

Free solar panels are another big thing. The local businesses don't stand a chance. I wish more NGOs and Aid organisations understood the effects their organisation has on local business and communities.

The latest buzzword is 'sustainable development' – helping the poor to educate themselves out of poverty, but the same donor principles apply. The Western world provides free training, machinery, grain, and builds free schools with volunteers working as teachers. Every time we give away something for free, we hamper a local business opportunity that would, if successful, provide jobs, pay salaries, and grow.

Big multinational companies have a huge advantage over local businesses with more knowledge, funds, and a working channel to market. If applied correctly, these advantages will result in local employment but many multinationals exploit local staff to produce the cheapest goods possible.

While building mobile networks in Africa I used experts from the head office in Holland, our resource office in South Africa, and external consultants from various companies. The internally sourced resources got a higher degree of freedom and management responsibility while the external resources were given more task-oriented, short-term roles. While not being better managers or more skilled in leadership, the internal resources shared the same long-term goal of building up our various mobile networks to the highest standard.

At Starfish Mobile, we have local individuals and companies as partners. We train the staff, supporting them in sales, business development and operational matters. Profit generation is our aim. We try to achieve this in a way that helps individuals and communities grow and prosper.

WHY NOT?

"Why are we doing this – dashing across the globe from client to client?" asked business strategist Nicola Tyler, frantically searching for some papers needed for her next trip. As CEO of the Business Results Group, she is constantly on a plane to a client meeting somewhere in the world.

"Why not?" I asked. It's a great question.

"Why not?" generates better answers and allows you to fill in the blanks using your gut feel. "Why not?" sounds positive and adventurous.

"Why not" has been my guiding principle throughout.

Were the social sacrifices worth it? YES! All my experiences have made me what I am today and I would not change that for a million bucks.

If you get the chance, take it! Go forth and explore. Experience. Learn. Enjoy every second!

The only failure is never trying. I like to think I succeeded but more importantly, it's been a fantastic journey!

RECOMMENDED READING

Hofstede, G: "Cultures and Organizations: Software of the Mind. Revised and expanded 3rd Edition" published by McGraw-Hill USA, 2010. The definitions and dimension scores used in this book are copyright by Geert Hofstede B.V. and quoted with permission.

Trompenaars F, Hampden-Turner C: "Riding the waves of culture: Understanding Cultural Diversity in Business. Second Edition" first published by Nicholas Brealey Publishing, 1997

Branson, R: "Losing My Virginity. The Autobiography" published by Virgin Books Ltd, 2005

Phillips-Martinsson, J: "Swedes as other see them. Revised second edition" published by Studentlitteratur, 1991

Bengtsson, Frans G.: "The Long Ships: A Saga of the Viking Age" published by HarperCollins Publishers, 1994

Steele, J: "War Junkie: One Man's Addiction to the Worst Places on Earth" published by Transworld, 2002